Wilfried Müller

111

PORSCHE STORIES THAT YOU SHOULD KNOW

emons:

Contents

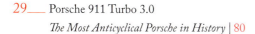

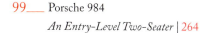

Foreword

A book full of Porsche stories. Not a history book, and not a work of reference – but 111 crisp and delicious stories to amaze you, to make you smile, to delight you. And if many of you say, after reading one of these tales, "Well, I didn't know that!", then that would make me very happy. It goes without saying that a book about Porsche has to tell stories about people. About the founding father Ferdinand, a self-taught man and a design genius. About the Ferdinands who followed him: Ferry invented the Porsche sports car, F. A. designed the 911, and Ferdinand Piëch continued the tradition of technical revolutionaries. Many people in the background guided the destiny of the world's most famous maker of sports cars. They stood at drawing boards, and in the pits on racing tracks around the globe. Brilliant masters of their trade, superb and cunning motor-sports strategists, and characters with extremely interesting stories. Of course the book is also about racing drivers – those daredevils of the universe of speed – and about the tracks on which they duelled for victory, where they wrote chapters of triumph and defeat.

"Porsche" means "car" – a very special kind of car. Our stories tell of the first electric-powered vehicle, more than a century ago; of milestones in sports-car history; of birds of paradise and prototypes; of racing cars that won, that lost, that never entered a race or were made by hand in tiny numbers as family treasures. Porsche is associated with magic words, some well known, others less known. It was fascinating to find out what lies behind those words: Gmünd, Turbo, Carrera, Speedster ...

Finally, this book is about special moments, such as when a Porsche plummeted to the ground from a considerable height, and the first crash test had been completed. Or when two Porsche 917s finished a 1,000-kilometre race in four hours, and were only four tenths of a second apart at the chequered flag. Warm thanks for expert and infinitely patient help are due to Dieter Landenberger, head of the Historic Archive in the Porsche Museum in Stuttgart-Zuffenhausen, to Jens Torner, the image archivist there, and his colleague Tobias Mauler.

And now I cordially invite you to set out on a fascinating journey to the world of Porsche, and hope you enjoy the 111 stages of the trip.

Wilfried Müller

In 1922 Ferdinand Porsche designed the Austro Daimler "Sascha" ADS R – a revolutionary racing car, small, light and nimble, with a 1.1-litre engine and 45 hp.

EARLY YEARS

1— The Lohner-Porsche Electromobile

Faster than a Gallop

The year is 1899. Technology fever has taken hold. The automobile is catapulting this generation to intoxicating speeds beyond a horse's gallop. Young technicians are tinkering at various power sources: gas, petrol, electricity. Ferdinand Porsche, a 23-year-old self-taught designer, has taken a job at Jakob Lohner's "royal and imperial court carriage works", in Vienna, and brought along a precious gift. He has devised and patented a steerable electric wheel-hub motor to power a car. It is practically silent, it doesn't stink, and it usually works.

Diverse forms of electric powering existed, but none required as little wiring and as few electrical connections, and none saved the labour of designing complicated means of transmission, because Porsche's invention put the power right on the wheel. In the year that Porsche joined him, Lohner decided to venture the making of an automobile. And to employ the design of the young technician from Bohemia, because the air was being " ... mercilessly ruined by the appearance of great numbers of petrol engines", in Lohner's words as quoted by the Vienna Technical Museum.

In 1899, by combining two wheel-hub motors on the steered front axle with a carriage chassis, the Lohner-Porsche electromobile was created. In 1900 Lohner exhibited Porsche's construction at the world fair in Paris. The vehicle, with 2.5 hp or 1.8 kW on each front wheel, was enthusiastically received. It could easily run at 35 km/h, and was claimed to be capable of 50 km/h. But obstacles remained to be overcome to make it fit for everyday use. The lead battery weighing over eight cwt was exhausted after 50 kilometres at most, and the rubber tyres groaned under the weight of the 1.2-tonne vehicle. Young Ferdinand was already planning a remedy: the battery could be made smaller and charged by a generator as the car drove ...

—— The Lohner-Porsche electromobile on the Austrian stand at the Paris world fair in 1900. The back tyres are groaning under the weight of the lead battery.

2__ The Lohner-Porsche Semper Vivus

Ancestor of Hybrids

At the Paris world fair of 1900, the 24-year-old designer Ferdinand Porsche impressed the public with his Lohner-Porsche electromobile. However, the carriage powered by two wheel-hub motors was hampered by its modest range of 50 kilometres at best. While his contemporaries were still looking on with amazement in Paris, Porsche's genius gave birth to further innovations in automobile history in Vienna: a racing car with electric motors and brakes on every wheel – both of these a world premiere. And his "Semper Vivus" became the first-ever working hybrid car.

To keep the Semper Vivus "always alive", as its name says, Ferdinand combined two small, water-cooled De Dion Bouton single-cylinder engines of 750 cc capacity and 3.5 hp (2.6 kW) with one generator each. The generators supplied 20 amps at 90 volts to a wheel-hub motor on each front wheel, mobilising 2.5 hp (1.8 kW). Surplus power from the generators charged the lead battery. Now having only 44 cells, it was much smaller than the 74-cell monster from the electric vehicle. Thanks to the hybrid technology, its range expanded to around 200 kilometres – not yet "semper vivus", but a huge step forward. Having the car's own "charging station" proved to be a brilliant idea for the future. Some fine tuning, especially on the interaction of the internal combustion engine, generators and battery, was needed to make it ready for series production. Finally Porsche presented the "Lohner-Porsche Mixte", a hybrid car with a four-cylinder front engine and wheel-hub motors, the basis for a small series of hybrid automobiles.

___ A topless, hybrid-powered automobile in the style of the dawning century: Porsche's Semper Vivus with electric motors at the front and combustion engines in front of the back passengers' knees.

3_ "Sascha", the Austro-Daimler Racing Car

Small, Light and Fast

Ferdinand Porsche was 31 years old when he became technical director of the Österreichische Daimler Motoren Gesellschaft – Austro Daimler for short – in the town of Wiener Neustadt in 1906. The following years were successful, as Porsche designed buses, fire engines, racing cars, aircraft engines and, during the First World War, military equipment. He was so effective at this that the Vienna Technical University awarded him an honorary doctorate in 1917.

Two ideas continued to obsess Porsche: motor racing and a relatively small, affordable car (which had to be made known by means of motor racing). In 1922 Porsche put this idea into practice by designing a small racing car – a revolutionary idea in an age when cars, as luxury products, were expected to be prestigious, large and powerful. Porsche's philosophy, by contrast, was to be smaller, lighter and thus faster. Austro Daimler rejected the idea, so Porsche's friend Count Alexander Joseph (Sascha) Kolowrat-Krakowsky – a racing driver and film producer – helped out with a loan. Porsche named his sporty little car Austro-Daimler ADS R "Sascha".

Four Saschas stood at the starting line in 1922 for one of the leading racing events: the Targa Florio in Sicily. Porsche's fastest man was his test driver Alfred Neubauer, later head of racing at Mercedes. Over the 432 kilometres Neubauer drove his Sascha at an average speed of 54 km/h to finish in 19th place. With his 1.1-litre, four-cylinder engine, Neubauer was only eight km/h slower than a 4.5-litre Mercedes! Two other Saschas completed the race, while Count Sascha himself dropped out with a technical fault. The little racer had several more successes, one of them on the fast track at Spa in Belgium, where a Sascha competed with covered spoke wheels and a water-drop-shaped rear. In 1923 the restless genius Porsche left Austro Daimler for the Daimler Motorengesellschaft in Untertürkheim, Stuttgart, where he took up a position on the board of management.

___ The Sascha competing in a race in Graz in 1922. To the left of the car is the well-fed sponsor, Count Kolowrat. On the right, wearing a stiff collar, is Ferdinand Porsche with his son Ferry.

4__ Auto Union Grand Prix Racing Car

A Model for Modern Motor Sports

In the early 1930s Mercedes-Benz dominated in Grand Prix motor sport. The Auto Union, a merger of the car makes Audi, DKW, Horch and Wanderer, pushed its way into this sport, which was prestigious and therefore strongly promoted by the Nazis. From 1932 the 750-kilogram rule applied to Grand Prix cars: a maximum weight designed to prevent ever bigger and ever more powerful one-seater cars. The situation was ideal for Ferdinand Porsche and his creed of "smaller + lighter = faster".

With the help of racing driver Hans Stuck – a superstar of the time – Auto Union was successful in raising money to develop an Auto Union racing car. On 17 March 1933 the task was given to Porsche, and in early summer the first Type 22 Auto Union P (for Porsche) was made in the racing department of Auto Union in Zwickau. A sixteen-cylinder V engine with 4.4 litres capacity and a Roots compressor generated 295 hp, passed to the back axle via a five-gear transmission. In contrast to the opposition, the car had its engine in front of the rear axle, which made for a good balance of weight and cornering speeds.

Hans Stuck dominated the 1934 racing season with the P car, set three world records, and became German hill-climbing champion. The following year Stuck and Bernd Rosemeyer, who had joined the team, fought a bitter struggle for prestige with the car. In 1936 Rosemeyer became European champion, then the highest-ranking title in Grand Prix racing, with the help of the Porsche design. One year later Mercedes was victorious, but Rosemeyer, in the Auto Union racer with aerodynamics developed by Porsche, was the first man to drive faster than 400 km/h. His exact speed on the Autobahn to Frankfurt was 406.3 km/h. Until December 1937 Ferdinand Porsche remained the leading figure in developing this racing car – and its mid-engine concept has been part of motor sports ever since.

___ The Type 22 was fitted with a cockpit for record-breaking attempts in 1937. Ferdinand Porsche, his back to the camera, watches the approach of his car.

Superstars of their age: Hans Stuck in white racing overalls, behind him Ferdinand Porsche next to the Auto Union GP racing car in Brno, now in the Czech Republic, in 1933.

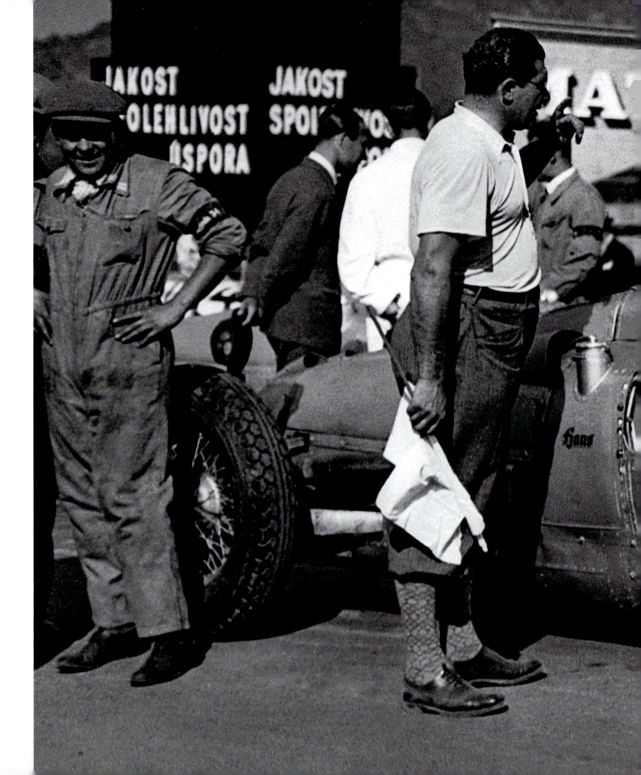

— The patriarch Ferry Porsche standing in front of one of his racing cars in 1968. On the right his sons F.A. (far right) and Hans-Peter, on the left his nephew Ferdinand Piëch.

KEY FIGURES

5_ Ferdinand Porsche

The Legend Begins

The Porsche legend starts with Ferdinand Porsche, who was born on 3 September 1875 in Maffersdorf in Bohemia (today Vratislavice in the Czech Republic) and died on 30 January 1951 in Stuttgart. He was to have been a plumber, but the new source of power, electricity, fascinated him. He rode to evening school on a humming electric bike that he made himself, a self-taught genius who did everything differently from that time onwards: a wheel-hub motor instead of complex power transmission for his electromobile in 1900, then hybrid powering, then small, light racing cars like his "Sascha" instead of big-engine giants; then the Mercedes S, SS and SSK sports cars. Wherever Porsche worked, his career moved forwards at racing speed: Austro-Daimler, Daimler Motor Company, Steyr. Usually his employment ended in a dispute: his designs seemed too elaborate for some and he had a fiery temperament.

In 1931 he had had enough of thinking for other bosses. In Kronenstrasse in Stuttgart he founded his own design office with a team of brilliant engineers like Erwin Komenda, Karl Rabe and Franz Xaver Reimspiess. Kronen-strasse was the birthplace of the mid-engine, synchroniser rings, torsion bar suspension – an endless list of innovations. The Auto Union "Silver Arrow" was designed there, as well as small cars for NSU and Zündapp: round-shaped, rear engines, one of them a boxer engine. In 1934 he was commissioned to design the "Volkswagen". In 1935 the first prototypes were tested. Then war broke out, and Porsche designed Kübelwagen and tanks.

After the end of the war he was imprisoned by the French for 22 months, fell seriously ill, was released in August 1947 and rehabilitated by court in 1948, and saw the success story of his Volkswagen "Beetle". In the same year, his son Ferry put the first Porsche 356 on the road. Small, light and sporty – just the style of his father Ferdinand.

___ Ferdinand Porsche in 1934 in a typical pose: with a stop-watch in his hand he checks the times of his racing drivers.

6_ Ferdinand "Ferry" Porsche

"I started by looking around ..."

Ferdinand Anton Ernst "Ferry" Porsche turned his famous father's design office into a world-famous sports car manufacturer. But let's begin at the beginning.

Aloisia Porsche brought Ferry into the world on 19 September 1909 in the town of Wiener Neustadt, while his father was driving in a race. Like the father, the only son rushed through his apprenticeship at top speed. After school he had a year's internship at Bosch, then a year at Steyr. Then came the drawing board. From 1931 he worked in his father's company, where the two of them landed their great coup in 1934: the commission to design the Volkswagen. The fact that the powerful but jealous Reich Automobile Industry Association gave a positive rating to Porsche's hand-made Beetle prototypes after extremely tough tests is testimony firstly to their design quality and secondly to Ferry's excellent diplomatic skills, as the association feared competition for its own cars. After the war Ferry negotiated the contract with Volkswagen that secured Porsche's financial future. And then: "I started by looking around, but I couldn't find the car that I was dreaming of: a small, light sports car that used energy efficiently. So I decided to make it myself." The 356/1 of 1948 was the first sports car to carry the Porsche name. 500 sports cars a year could be sold, according to Ferry's estimate. By 1965 the figure had exceeded 78,000. In the mid-1960s he charted a new course and pushed through a sports-car design by his eldest son, Ferdinand Alexander: the 911.

In 1972 Ferry Porsche and the family decided to leave business operations to managers in future, and the company Porsche AG was created. As head of the supervisory board he watched over the board members until 1990 – quietly and diplomatically, the way he always acted. Ferry Porsche died on 27 March 1998 in Zell am See.

___ Ferry Porsche in Le Mans in 1961, when a tie and hat were still worn at races. Ferdinand Porsche's son is regarded as the father of the 356 – and of the Porsche sports-car marque.

7__ Louise Piëch

Steering Porsche through Times of Crisis

For her 70th birthday in 1974, Ferry Porsche gave his sister Louise Piëch the first 911 Turbo. The present and the birthday girl were a good match. The Turbo stands for power and impetuosity – it was a Porsche that some found frightening. Which is a good description of some of the characteristics of Ferdinand Porsche's only daughter.

She studied painting and had a lifelong devotion to the arts. In 1928 Louise Porsche married the lawyer Anton Piëch, with whom she had four children. In the war years and the post-war period Louise Piëch proved to be an excellent leader of the company. Even before the company moved to Carnatia in 1944, she took drawings and equipment to Austria. When her father, brother and husband were interned after the war ended, she managed the base in Gmünd in cooperation with the chief engineer, Karl Rabe. In November 1946 Ferry was released from imprisonment by the French, and a month later a major contract was gained. The earnings were enough to pay bail of one million francs, freeing Ferdinand Porsche and Anton Piëch from imprisonment. Louise made her next successful move on 1 April 1947: as the occupying powers were confiscating the property of German companies, she and her brother founded an Austrian company, Porsche Konstruktionen GmbH, in Gmünd. Here, with Louise and Ferry as managing directors, the first Porsche sports cars were made. From 1949 Louise and Anton Piëch's company Porsche Salzburg GmbH was the exclusive Austrian importer of Volkswagen cars. After the death of her husband she continued to manage the company, which under the ownership of the Porsche and Piëch families became the biggest European car dealer and was soon operating successfully in Asia.

The most important woman in the Porsche story died in 1999 in Zell am See. One of her sons helped to guide the sports-car manufacturer into the 21st century: Ferdinand Piëch.

___ Louise Piëch played a decisive part in the survival of the Porsche company in the post-war period. She was one of the leading entrepreneurial personalities in Europe.

8_ Ferdinand Alexander "F. A." Porsche

Designer of the 911

"Porsche Design" – every air passenger knows the airport shops of this high-end design company, founded by Ferdinand Alexander Porsche in 1972. Today, however, Porsche Design means not only exclusive accessories, but also pioneering industrial design. The way forward was laid down by "F. A." in a number of interviews: function is the alpha and omega, the core of form. No playful nuances, but reduction to what is feasible and sensible. In the very best quality, it goes without saying.

Ferry Porsche's eldest son, known as "Butzi" in the family, was born on 11 December 1935 and first started work in his father's company in late 1957. He had just been expelled from design school in Ulm after one semester. "… I assume that my behaviour was not sufficiently diplomatic in the web of leading authorities", he told "Christophorus" magazine in 1998. F. A. made drawings for single-seater racing cars, including the famous "Three-Edged Scraper", a racer with a cabin roof that seemed to have been sliced off behind the driver. The debate about a successor to the 356 model was running at maximum revs, and here, too, F. A. played his part. In 1961 he presented his T8, with a design that was preferred to those produced by Graf Goertz (BMW 507) and Erwin Komenda. Goertz was a star designer, Komenda an important man at Porsche who had been in charge of the bodywork department since 1931. F. A.: "I wanted to create a completely neutral car without anything fancy. A modern car, not a fashionable one." In May 1962, F. A. Porsche's successful design was given the type number 901, and its success story began. A year later, with the 904 Carrera GTS, F. A. turned out a further classic sports-car design.

In 1990 he was appointed chairman of the supervisory board of Porsche AG, and a year later became honorary chairman. F. A. Porsche died on 5 April 2012.

___ We've done it! The new 901 is on wheels, and designer F. A. Porsche (right) poses in 1964 with the sports car that was to epitomise Porsche.

9__ Wolfgang Porsche

Powerful, but not Power-Hungry

He is the man with the same name as the cars and the company: Porsche. Dr Wolfgang Porsche. Born in 1943, a grandson, son and father of the Porsche line. A passionate hunter. A farmer at the family seat, Schüttgut near Zell am See. An aesthete, an art collector, a businessman with petrol running through his veins, an ambassador for automobiles "made in Germany". Chairman of the supervisory board of Porsche AG and Porsche Auto-mobil Holding SE, member of the supervisory board of Volkswagen AG and Audi AG.

A man with a great deal of power. Yet no lover of power. Many describe him as the quiet heart of the Porsche-Piëch clan – the most influential automobile dynasty in Europe. A man for whom the heads of managers and media representatives turn respectfully at motor shows in Geneva, Detroit and Frankfurt. Wolfgang Porsche, the face of an empire, whom Porsche fans all over the world encounter with high esteem and requests for selfies when he turns up at motor-sports and veteran-car events like the Mille Miglia.

The youngest of four sons, he is regarded as the torch-bearer for what those automobile pioneers, his father Ferry and grandfather Ferdinand, established: the world's most successful sports car marque. WoPo, as he is called in the company, does everything possible to preserve this inheritance. Since the death of Ferry Porsche he has been the family spokesman. A rich man who is also trusted by ordinary people. In one of his darkest hours, 23 July 2009, when the pack had to be reshuffled in the takeover battle for Volkswagen and the chairman of the Porsche executive board, Dr Wendelin Wiedeking, had to leave the helm, Wolfgang Porsche told his employees: "Don't worry about your jobs. Our prospects are good. And trust me: the Porsche legend lives on and will never die." He was proved right – today Porsche is stronger than ever before.

___ The friendly face of an automobile concern: many regard Ferry Porsche's son Wolfgang as the quiet heart of the Porsche-Piëch clan.

10_ Ferdinand Piëch

A Visionary and Shaper

Ferdinand Karl Piëch: Ferdinand Porsche's grandson, born in 1937 in Vienna to Louise (née Porsche) and Anton Piëch. He went to boarding school, studied engineering and wrote his thesis about Formula 1 engines. In 1963 he joined the test department at Porsche, where he showed considerable talent, including the ability to use his elbows. By 1965 he was already head of development, and in motor sports took the firm from class winner to champion.

His ways were radical: the racing cars were always close to the minimum permitted weight. They were streamlined and fast – so fast and unruly that even hard-bitten drivers said "no thank you". For the works team Piëch engaged the best drivers. He equipped several teams with his 917 super-racer, according to the motto "competition improves the lap times". In 1969 Porsche was world champion, in 1970 and 1971 again. Observers were already speculating that this energetic visionary had his eyes on the top job at Zuffenhausen, but then the Porsche and Piëch families withdrew from an operative role. Piëch went to Audi, then to Volkswagen. He turned both companies on their heads. His legacy included the Quattro and light-weight aluminium design, the TDI, one-litre cars and a 1,000-hp Bugatti. With Piëch as chairman, Volkswagen was soon on the way to becoming the world's biggest car marque. Then Porsche tried to take over Volkswagen. Piëch possibly saw this as an attack on his position, and struck back. His influence runs all the way to the top in Zuffenhausen: Porsche boss Wiedeking had to leave. With a shudder of pleasure it was said that Piëch could topple a top manager with an aside to reporters.

Ferdinand Piëch officially laid down the burden of all his offices in 2015 but still watched events in the VW Group like a hawk. He passed away aged 82 in August 2019.

____ A pit stop for the powerful Porsche 917 at the 24 Hours of Le Mans in 1969. Ferdinand Piëch (right) initiated development of this future series winner.

11___ Helmuth Bott

A Director with a Heart

Among Porsche lovers the name Helmuth Bott triggers a chain of delightful associations. Born in Swabia in 1925, he came to Porsche in 1952 and was head of the test department at the time when the 911 was conceived. Under his aegis as director of development from 1978 to 1988, the first four-wheel-drive 911 and the 959 super sports car saw the light of day.

Those who know the company attribute unlimited creative energy to this self-made man, who did an apprenticeship as a mechanic from 1945 to 1947 and had to cut short his university course in engineering for lack of money. Bott developed pioneering test procedures, standardised driving trials, organised and planned the development centre at Weissach, initiated systematic crash tests and supported the development of the catalytic converter. He promoted motor sports with huge success – the mention of Le Mans, TAG Turbo and Paris–Dakar suffices to show this. His staff fondly remember their boss as "Father Bott", who liked open talking, calmed many a conflict, discovered and promoted talented employees, played cards in the evening with the team on test trips, and took everyone off to the cinema or a harbour pub. Who had a passion for ice-cream and got annoyed about wasted time if he had to wait three minutes at a petrol station. Uncompromising as Bott was when he insisted on completing the daily allotment of 1,000 kilometres during tests in the Sahara or the Canadian ice, even without air conditioning or heating in the car, he also took delight in a half-day trip for his test staff to the Table Mountain at Cape Town when they were in the area with a secret test car.

In 1985 Bott was honoured by the German government with its Bundesverdienstkreuz and made an honorary professor. In 1987 he was awarded an honorary doctorate. A year later Helmuth Bott retired. He died in 1994.

___ Helmuth Bott (second from right), who went from mechanic to board member for research at Porsche, was highly respected by his employees and affectionately known as "Father Bott".

12___ Ernst Fuhrmann

First Chairman of the Board, Promoter of Turbo

Ernst Fuhrmann was a Porsche man from the founding years. Born in Vienna in 1918 and trained at the Technical University, in 1947 he joined the design office in Gmünd and stayed with Porsche at Zuffenhausen. Until 1956 he was part of the small team that nurtured the 356. In 1950 Fuhrmann presented his doctoral thesis on "Camshaft Control of Fast-Running Combustion Engines" at Vienna Technical University and, as Dr Fuhrmann, designed his famous four-camshaft racing engine, known as the "Fuhrmann", "Carrera" or "Drawer" engine – the last term because, when visitors arrived during the secret design phase, all the parts vanished into a drawer at lightning speed.

Fuhrmann left Porsche in 1956 but returned in September 1971. The owners, the Porsche and Piëch families, converted their company to a joint-stock corporation. Their old associate Fuhrmann became the first spokesman of the executive board, and from November 1976 the first chairman of the Porsche board. He was a brilliant engineer and a far-sighted manager, a technician through and through who often put in an appearance in the test and design offices, and who masterfully guided Porsche through the "energy crisis" of the early 1970s with his finance director Branitzki. And then pulled off the coup of launching the then most expensive and powerful sports car in Porsche history, the 911 Turbo, in the middle of this crisis.

He was an energetic boss, and sometimes reacted with exasperation to references, even unintentional, to his Napoleonic physical stature. He was not above shedding tears of joy when Porsche won at Le Mans. Fuhrmann was convinced that the future lay in transaxle sports cars like the 924 or 928. Initially the owning families shared this opinion, but later departed from this view. The first chairman of the board and the families went different ways. At the end of 1980 Fuhrmann retired.

___ Ernst Fuhrman (right) designed the Carrera engine and was Porsche's first chairman of the board. The photo with racing driver Herbert Müller was taken in 1973 at Le Mans.

13__ Horst Marchart

A Quiet Helmsman Who Changed Course

It was a dramatic period when Horst Marchart took the position of head of research and development in October 1991. The dollar had nose-dived, and business in the USA, vital to Porsche, had imploded. The production of three completely different series of models was draining great amounts of cash, and the 928 and 944/968 transaxle sports cars had lost their popularity. At the same time the development costs of the Type 989 four-seater project went through the roof, until Porsche stopped it. Marchart's predecessor Ulrich Bez left the company, followed by chairman of the board Arno Bohn.

Marchart now occupied the ejector seat. Born in Vienna, he graduated in vehicle and engine technology and had been with Porsche for 30 years, most recently as head of overall vehicle development. Now, in a position that was the key to the future, he operated calmly and far-sightedly, with the ability to gain consensus. Together with the new chairman Wendelin Wiedeking and head of design Harm Lagaaij, Marchart turned things around. In autumn 1991 he initiated development of a mid-engine roadster – later the Boxster – and a new 911. Both had water-cooled engines and were 50 per cent made from the same parts – a huge break with the past for Porsche. The Boxster soon proved to be a success, and the strategy of using the same parts led to enormous savings in production. Yet Marchart did not make savings at all costs. Where the engine of the Boxster was concerned, in view of experience with the four-cylinder Porsche he insisted on a six-cylinder boxer engine, even in the face of opposition in the company.

By the time Marchart retired in March 2001 at the age of 62 he had put the Carrera GT super sports car and the Cayenne on course. Without ever appearing in the headlines. This a Porsche story that everyone should know.

____ Horst Marchart (right) cautiously steered Porsche through a decisive period as head of development. Here he is listening to his racing engineer Norbert Singer.

14__ Anatole Carl Lapine

G Series 911, Bestseller and Space Glider

On 15 April 1969, shortly before his 39th birthday, Latvian-born Anatole Carl Lapine moved into the boss's office at Porsche Style. He had a big pair of boots to fill. His predecessor was F. A. Porsche, creator of the 911 design.

The second 911 generation, the "G Series", came from Lapine's pen. He managed the tightrope walk of complying with US safety legislation by putting rubber buffers on the bumpers while still designing a fantastic 911. This was a great feat, and it lasted from 1973 to 1989, longer than any other 911. The design of the transaxle sports car – the Porsche with the engine at the front and the gearbox in front of the back axle – was also created under Lapine. The 924, the entry-level Porsche, was as controversial as it was successful. The great 928 raced ahead of the taste of the time. Only fans of an avant-garde appearance and forward-looking technology fell in love with this GT, which looked like a space glider. Today the 928 is a cult car.

Lapine, who in his fifties looked the way di Caprio might look later, was a nonconformist to the core. A British Lotus racing sports car stood in his office. Chairman of the board Fuhrmann accepted this as destiny: "These style people are artists, you have to give them some leeway." Even as a Porsche novice, Lapine had caused a stir with the 917 racing cars dubbed the "Hippie Car" and the "Sau".

Lapine remained Porsche's top stylist until 1988. Before joining the company he had spent some years in the USA. A trained car mechanic and graduate of the school of car making, Lapine started at General Motors in 1951. There he belonged to the team of the secretive "Studio X", where the Corvette SS (1957) and the XP-87 Stingray were created. Later Lapine developed racing car designs and was sent by GM to be head of design at Opel, where he produced his "Black Widow" despite a ban on racing from America. But that's another story.

___ Anatole Lapine (second from left) was head of Porsche Style and thus the top designer from 1969 to 1988. This photo was taken in about 1973 in Weissach.

15__ Harm Lagaaij

Who Dares, Wins

Porsche stylists have a tough job. The silhouette of the 911 is untouchable, but in its sixth decade has to be kept up to date – or even better, ahead of its time. In the early nineties the job of Harm Lagaaij, head of Porsche Style since 1989, was especially tricky: Porsche needed nothing less than a new start alongside the 911. The transaxle models no longer made fans' hearts throb. On top of this came the fall in the dollar and an economic crisis. Considered soberly, survival was at stake.

Lagaaij, born in the Netherlands, had been at Porsche in the seventies, then at BMW, among other companies. He returned to Weissach in 1989 and took a bold step. He immersed himself in the history, took the lines of the 550 Spyder and 718 RS 60 racing cars from the fifties and sixties, and drew up with his team a breath-taking interpretation of classic forms and proportions: a new mid-engine Porsche. What he and his colleagues created is all the more admirable for the fact that the new model had to correspond to the next 911 up to the B pillar. This had been worked out by Marchart, board member for development, and the new Porsche boss Wendelin Wiedeking.

Porsche presented the "Boxster" – a combination of the words "boxer" (for the engine) and roadster (for the joy of open-top driving) – on 5 January 1993 at the North American International Auto Show in Detroit. In the following weeks this little silver jewel, fitted with red-brown aniline leather, dominated the motoring pages of the world's newspapers. There was general enthusiasm, and Lagaaij sighed in relief. The door to the future had been kicked open. Lagaaij was later to handle the styling of the Cayman mid-engine coupé, the Carrera GT super sports car and the Cayenne, before handing over the drawing board to Michael Mauer in 2004.

____ A classic form in a modern look: Harm Lagaaij (centre), head of design, with his colleagues Grant Larson (left) and Matthias Kulla in the Weissach studio with a model of the 911.

16__ Michael Mauer

Porsche Style in the 21st Century

Every current Porsche is marked by the hand of Michael Mauer. Since 2004 he has guided the design of the sports cars. As the head of Porsche Style he leads a team of some 100 designers, model makers and CAD specialists that develops a typical vocabulary of form from countless interactions of tradition and fitness for the future, aesthetics, technology and business feasibility.

Mauer set the eighth generation of the 911 on its way, thus sharing the destiny of his predecessors in breeding this model for years ahead on the basis of its classic genes. He mastered the delicate operation of portraying the four-seater Panamera unmistakably as a Porsche – a very large car that could not be allowed to lose anything of the cutting edge of a sports car. Or the Cayman: quoting the wonderful 550, free of any dusty nostalgia, and clearly a Porsche. The Macan: a travelling sculpture, at repose within itself for all its dynamism and agility. The 918 Spyder, the Taycan ... the task is to retain the brand identity. It has to be clear at first sight that this is a Porsche. Yet nothing is as damaging as repetition of the same, unchanging thing. Product identity has to be created: this car is new, unmistakable and a Porsche that holds six decades of sports-car history. Whether the design of a sports car is successful depends on the right proportions – a creed that Mauer untiringly propagates. The line that he took was convincing. In December 2015 he became head of design for the whole VW group.

The start of all this was entirely harmless. Born in 1962 in the federal state of Hessen, Mauer grew up in the Black Forest, and always had two loves: drawing and cars. Well, three loves: sports were and remain a great passion. At university in Pforzheim Mauer studied transportation design. He spent many years at Mercedes-Benz, followed by periods at Saab and Advanced Design for GM, before his path led to Porsche.

___ Michael Mauer, head of design at Porsche from 2004, has had the same function for the whole Volkswagen group since 2015: "Everything depends on the proportions."

17__Wendelin Wiedeking

A New Broom Sweeps Clean

From 1 August 1992 until 23 July 2009, Dr Wendelin Wiedeking, a Westphalian engineer, managed Porsche as chairman of the executive board. The company was in the red when he took over at the age of 40. Then things moved: in 1995 the accounts showed a small profit, after a loss of 450 million deutschmarks the previous year.

Unconventional, uncompromising, unregarding of taboos or privileges, Wiedeking slimmed down production and created a lean management and dealerships. His extraordinary stamina – at work, parties, and wielding his new broom – was quickly as legendary as his strategic touch. The transaxle Porsche disappeared, the Boxster and Cayenne arrived, and the new factory in Leipzig worked flat out. Porsche grew, created jobs and posted record profits every year. In the ten years to August 2002, the share price rose by 1,739 per cent. Wiedeking's salary rose with it, as he had agreed to work without a fixed income. The Porsche and Piëch families would not part with common shares at that time, so Wiedeking accepted almost 0.9 per cent of earnings before tax as his salary.

In 2005 a coup started: the rich dwarf Porsche wanted to take over the giant VW. The ancient link between the two companies would have been secure. With the families' consent, Wiedeking went into action. In late October 2008 it was official, and the talk was of a "takeover battle": Wiedeking against the federal state of Lower Saxony, the shareholder with a blocking minority, against the workers' representatives at VW and against Ferdinand Piëch, head of the VW supervisory board, who seemingly thought he was becoming too powerful. And finally against the emerging economic crisis. This was too much, and the bold financing plans collapsed. VW turned the tables, Porsche became a brand in the group, and Wiedeking had to go. This hurt, but it may be a wonderful consolation that everyone with a Porsche share is richer than in 1992.

___ When this picture was painted in 2002, Wendelin Wiedeking had been head of Porsche for ten years and the share price had risen by over 1,700 per cent.

This is how modern times began at Porsche: a 901 coupé in an advertising photo from 1964. The wooden steering wheel identifies it is as an early example.

MILESTONES

18__ Porsche Type 7

The Birth of the Porsche Company

From 1930 Ferdinand Porsche gathered a team of top engineers around him in Stuttgart. It included such men as the later chief engineer Karl Rabe, the engine specialist Franz-Xaver Reimspiess and the bodywork expert Erwin Komenda. On 25 April 1931, the limited company "Dr. Ing. h.c. Ferdinand Porsche GmbH", named as a design office for the construction of engines and road, air and water vehicles, was registered at the address Kronenstrasse 24. Porsche had his own company for the first time.

The Wanderer Works in Chemnitz, which belonged to Auto Union, commissioned the company to develop a "1.5-litre engine with chassis". In Kronenstrasse they were in celebratory mood: following six designs, this seventh one – Type 7 – was the first one sold by the office. In 1931 the company developed the Wanderer W 21, which was powered by a newly conceived engine of light metal with six cylinders in-line, 1.7 litres capacity and 35 horsepower. The chassis consisted of a flat frame, while sheet metal on a wooden frame formed the four-door bodywork, whose design met with an enthusiastic reception. Wanderer adopted several formal elements of the Porsche design for other models, too. Beneath the metal exterior lay several Porsche patents. On 10 August his office had patented torsion bar suspension – a brilliant and space-saving solution that was even to reappear in the 911 model. The car, hugely advanced for its time, was also characterised by compact screw-and-nut steering and the option of ordering Trilok automatic gears.

Orders now came pouring in to Porsche's design office. In September work started on a compact rear-engine car for Zündapp, the shape of which was somehow reminiscent of a bug. However, this car got no further than the prototype stage, as Zündapp decided to concentrate entirely on making motorcycles.

____ The design of the Type 7 aroused enthusiasm, as the car was packed with technical innovations such as torsion bar suspension, spindle steering and Trilok automatic gears.

19__ The Beetle and Porsche

One Idea, Two Legends

There would have been no Beetle without Porsche. And no Porsche sports car without the Beetle. This is how the story began: in 1933 a "Volkswagen", i.e. a people's car, was called for, costing 990 reichsmarks. 1.5 million were to be made per year. Car manufacturers, joined together in the Reich Association for the Automobile Industry, thought both of these conditions impossible and disliked the project, which threatened to compete with its own small cars. Ferdinand Porsche, however, did not make cars, was a world-famous designer, and had long been keen on the idea of a compact, low-cost automobile.

On 17 January 1934 Porsche presented his "exposé concerning the construction of a German people's car": a round shape, a boxer engine at the back, rear-wheel drive, torsion bar suspension. On 22 June 1934 his office received the enormous commission of designing the Volkswagen. From 1936 test drives with the "Type 60" took place, and for its production Porsche designed an automotive plant with a capacity never before known in Europe. 1938 saw the world premiere of the "Kraft durch Freude" ("strength through joy") car, as it was now named. Reporting on 3 July, the New York Times called it a "beetle". In 1939 Hitler plunged the world into war. Instead of the Beetle, the KdF factory in Fallersleben, directed by Porsche's son-in-law Anton Piëch, made army cars and other military hardware.

Only after the war did production of the Beetle, to be manufactured in greater numbers than any other car worldwide, begin in Wolfsburg, as the town was renamed in the summer of 1945. Porsche initially made an agreement with Volkswagen on a licence fee for each Beetle, an enormous boost to his new sports car firm. A few hundred kilometres to the south, in Gmünd, the first Porsche 356 was made, with an air-cooled boxer engine at the rear, back-wheel drive and torsion bar suspension: the car's ancestor lived on in a sports vehicle.

____ Ferdinand Porsche in Vienna in 1940 with a Beetle test car. Due to the war-time blackout, the headlights have been covered.

20__ Porsche 356 Number 1

The First Prototype

A reminder: because of bombing raids on Stuttgart, in November 1944, on the orders of Reich Minister Albert Speer, the Porsche office moved to Gmünd in Austria, in the Alpine foothills of Carnatia. Here, after the end of the war, with his father still imprisoned by the French, Ferry Porsche designed the revolutionary Cisitalia Formula 1 Monoposto – and the very first Porsche 356. Chief designer Karl Rabe and Erwin Komenda, head of the bodywork department, collaborated with Ferry on the prototype. Drawings dated 17 July 1947 show the "VW two-seater sports car", and the numbering on the right of the sheets starts with the legendary "356-001".

With a steel space frame, a mid-engine and aluminium bodywork, the Number 1 embodies racing-car philosophy at its purest. It was powered by a Beetle engine with 1.131 cc capacity from which the people at Porsche extracted 35 hp thanks to newly designed cylinder heads and fine tuning. The Number 1 weighed a mere 585 kilograms and could reach 135 km/h – if the driver dared: the steering, chassis and gears were plain and simple Volkswagen components.

On 8 June 1948 the Carnatian authorities gave their blessing to the 356-001 on the basis of inspection of an individual model, and on 1 July Ferdinand Porsche's nephew Herbert Kaes drove this light-weight to victory in his class at the Innsbruck races. So far, so good. But a mid-engine sports car with a space frame is far too expensive for series production. And no one knows how long a space frame deriving from motor sports will hold up. There was no point in looking for luggage space in this thoroughbred sports car, and in terms of styling, the folding roof in its closed position could justifiably be described as a slap in the face. But there was already a solution for all of this: Ferry and his team were working flat out on the 356/2.

____ How it all started: the Porsche 356 Number 1, made in 1948, remained a one-off but it marks the start of Porsche's success story as a sports car marque.

21_ Porsche 356/2

A Small Series of Gems

For a small band of hard-core Porsche fans, the only true sports cars come not from Zuffenhausen in Stuttgart (recently also from Leipzig, and in-between times from Uusikaupunki) but from Gmünd in the Austrian federal state of Carnatia. This is where, in spring 1948, the first Porsche sports cars came in any significant numbers: the 356/2 "Aluminium" or "Light Metal" or "Gmünd", just as you please.

Following Porsche's move to the relative safety of Austria in 1944 to avoid air raids on Stuttgart, a workforce of almost 300 designed and made winches, wind generators, tractors, a Formula 1 car and the 356 Number 1 prototype. On 1 April 1948 the decision was taken to make a small series of sports cars that differed, however, from the strange model that bore the number 1. Instead of the expensive, complex space frame, the chassis was a box-section frame. The 1,131 cc Beetle engine tuned to 40 hp was now positioned behind the rear axle, thus creating space for rumble seats or luggage. More comfortable means heavier. The 356/2 came in at a good two hundredweight more than the 356-001 prototype. In Gmünd there were highly skilled designers, mechanics and metalworkers for making the chassis, but no coachwork makers were available, so small specialised firms such as Kastenhofer, Keibl and Tatra in Vienna and Beutler in Switzerland built the hand-made aluminium bodies.

The first series-produced Porsche was given its public premiere at the Geneva Motor Show in spring 1949 – and was ecstatically acclaimed. Approximately five sports cars per month left the small factory in Gmünd. Following completion of eight 356/2 cabriolets and 44 356/2 limousines, production came to an end on 20 March 1950, while in Stuttgart-Zuffenhausen the first successors to these were already coming off the line by 6 April.

___ A 356/2 in Gmünd, where Porsche's first small series of sports cars was manually produced.

A seldom-seen rear view of the first series-produced Porsche: a 356/2 of 1948. Only 44 of these "limousines" were made in Gmünd.

22__ The Carrera Engine

Like a Racehorse – Complex and Fast

It was not possible to go on for ever with souped-up Beetle engines. In the early 1950s Porsche got 95 hp out of a harmless 1.6-litre pushrod engine. But that was the limit. Porsche needed an engine of its own, and typically did this for racing first. Ernst Fuhrmann gained his doctorate at Vienna Technical University in 1950 with a thesis about "Camshaft Control of Fast-Running Combustion Engines". The doctor entered the service of Porsche and developed an engine. In April 1953 Type 547 was running in tests, and in August it first operated in a car during practice at the German Grand Prix.

Porsche's first proprietary engine built in any quantities was an air-cooled four-cylinder boxer engine with a capacity of 1,498 cc and four camshafts at the top that were controlled by two upright shafts. The crank case, the cylinder heads and the pistons were made from light metal, while the running surfaces were chrome-hardened. Double carburettors and double ignition put the finishing touches on this high-performance package, and a dry sump ensured lubrication in long curves. This small four-cylinder motor is complex: it takes 120 hours to make one. However, it packs a punch: 110 hp at 7,800 rpm, but the machine can only really be driven at between 5,000 and 7,000 revs.

The "Fuhrmann engine" quickly became a guarantee of winning. Porsche soon also put it into especially fast and expensive 356 models, and now called both the engine and the sports car "Carrera". This engine stayed on the road to victory for a decade. In the Porsche 718 around 1957 it generated 150 horsepower. Between the late fifties and mid-sixties in the Porsche RS60 and RS61 – now with 1.6 litres capacity – it produced some 160 horsepower. Its peak performance came in the two-litre Type 587, which conjured up an astonishing 180 hp and from 1964 onwards powered the 904 GTS, among other models, to countless triumphs.

___ The "Fuhrmann engine", later known as the "Carrera engine", turned this 550 Spyder of 1953 into a rocket with its 110 hp and 1.5 litres capacity.

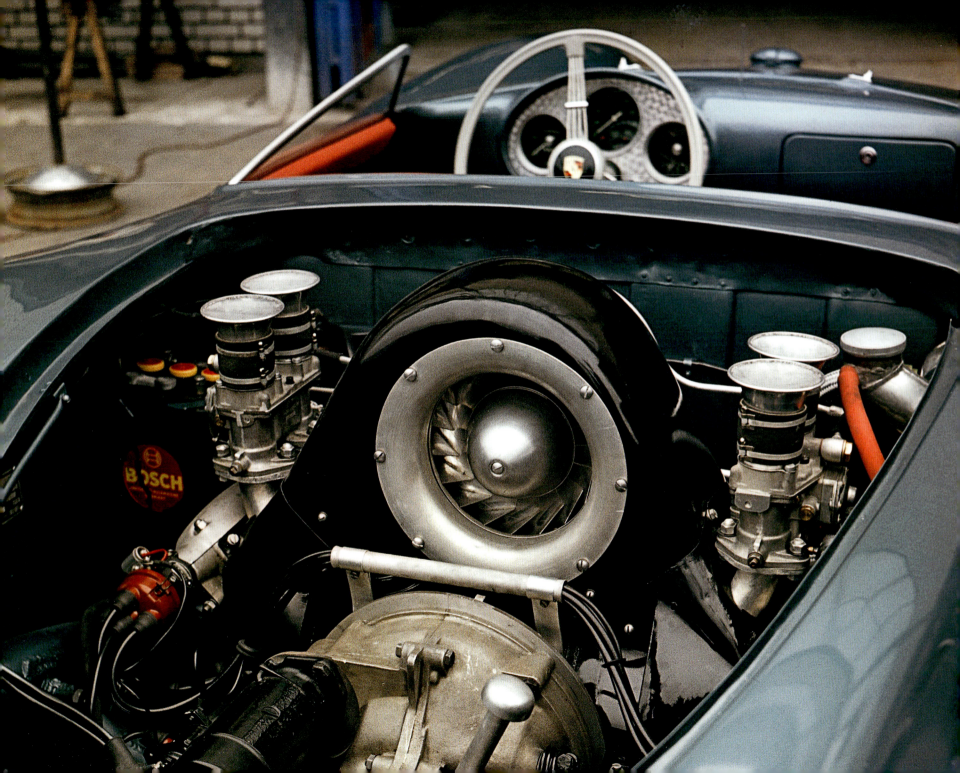

23_The Porsche 550 Spyder

A Mid-Engine Carriage

If this is not a milestone, what is? In 1953, the 550 Spyder became Porsche's first mid-engine sports car to be made in considerable numbers (90) – and the first to be named after the English word for a light carriage, "Spyder". In front of the rear axle was a newly designed racing engine that was to be a winner on the track until the early 1960s. It was the four-cylinder boxer engine designed by Dr Ernst Fuhrmann, with four camshafts driven by upright shafts. In a 550 Spyder, Hans Herrmann took third place in the Carrera Panamericana in 1954 – a superb achievement, which is why the engine was called the "Carrera engine" from that time onwards.

The 550 Spyder was extremely popular with amateur racing drivers. James Dean had one, which was involved in a fatal accident on 30 September 1955. Another car rammed the Porsche, and the actor was dead on the spot. In 1956 the new 550A Spyder appeared, with more power, a lighter space frame instead of the old flat frame, and bigger brakes. The 550A – of which 40 were produced – also made history: in 1956 the Italian driver Umberto Maglioli took this lightweight racer to the first victory for a Porsche at the world-famous Targa Florio.

It goes without saying that, along with the history, there are stories to be told. For example the story of the Dutch aristocrat Carel Godin de Beaufort, who had his 550A taken to New York by sea in 1958 so that he could take part in the 12 Hours of Sebring. Sebring is down in Florida, however, and the noble gentleman had left himself short of time. As a result, de Beaufort rapidly moved south along the east coast. Too rapidly, in the opinion of the sheriffs in two backwoods towns, who put him in jail twice. The bail money was paid from his petty cash, and he actually made it down to Sebring in time for the start – then had to retire from the race after 106 laps with a broken clutch.

___ A mouth-watering collection of 550 Spyders in 1956 in the yard of factory no. 1 in Stuttgart-Zuffenhausen. Those who visit Porsche today will easily recognise the factory yard.

24__ Porsche 911 2.0

The First Lines of the Legend

On 12 September 1963 the small company from Stuttgart-Zuffenhausen showed its new rear-engine sports car at the IAA International Automobile Exhibition in Frankfurt for the first time. The successor to the 356 sported the number 901, was a 2+2-seater and was powered by an air-cooled, six-cylinder boxer engine with two litres capacity, racing-style dry-sump lubrication and 130 horsepower. The chassis, too, was brand new, with McPherson suspension struts at the front and a semi-trailing arm axle. Ferdinand Alexander Porsche and his Porsche Style studio provided the bodywork design, which has remained to this day. It has the round headlights in the front wings, between which the luggage-space lid slopes like a low-lying valley. And it has the broad shoulders around the back axle, the fastback and the unique line of the side windows.

The first 901 to roll off the production line in Zuffenhausen left the factory on 14 September 1964. After making 82 cars, Porsche renamed the 901: it became the 911, as Peugeot had secured the rights to three-digit model designations with a zero in the middle. The new Porsche swept spirited sports-car fans off their feet, as the 911 is a car for drivers. One reason for this is that at Porsche the racing cars for the track and the sports cars for the road were made by the same people. Racing drivers like Eugen Böhringer, Herbert Linge and Hans Herrmann hammered the rear-engine machines around circuits at competition speeds until the handling suited them. With the consequence that those who want to drive fast in a 911 had better know what they are doing.

Today, more than half a century and seven 911 generations later, the car is like a mobile concentration of proven Swabian craftsmanship, technical know-how and delight in high performance, merging to form a sports car that keeps its promises to the driver.

___ A very early prototype of the Porsche 911 in the factory yard: the 901-1, in 1963. On the right in the background stands factory no. 1, on the left the hall with the engine testbeds.

25__ Porsche 911R

The First Racer in the 911 Series

"In our enthusiasm for light-weight construction, perhaps we overdid things with plastic. Whatever – there was a lot of rattling and shaking on the car". This is how Porsche's chief racing engineer Peter Falk remembered the 911R, the first racing 911, which was born in 1967 with the vigorous assistance of the young Ferdinand Piëch.

The doors, lids and covers, front wings and bumpers were made from thin plastic. The side and back windows were made from Plexiglas two millimetres thick, the windscreen from four-millimetre glass. For the first time a Porsche ran on light-metal wheels produced by Fuchs in Meinerzhagen, which soon acquired cult status as "Fuchs rims". The rear wings became moderately broader to make space for the 185-H15 tyres. In the cockpit things were spartan – Porsche did not even provide an ashtray, although the driver could do with a calming cigarette now and then: the 911R, weighing only 820 kilograms, set off like a rocket. Simmering at the back was a two-litre racing engine that not only looked fantastic, with its six open inlet funnels and two triple carburettors, but also generated 210 hp at 8,000 rpm and an unbeatable acoustic feast. Like all Porsches, this prize machine was lubricated from a dry sump. Beneath the door side sills, two oil pipes ran to two coolers at the front. Depending on the gearing, the 911R could get up to 230 km/h.

In the very same year when it was presented, the 911R set several world records in Monza, including covering 25,000 kilometres non-stop (with the exception of refuelling stops) in terrible weather at an average speed of 208.3 km/h. A number of competition wins and championships followed, especially at rallying. Porsche made 23 of this model. Four of them stayed in the factory and 19 were sold – for 45,000 deutschmarks each.

___ In 1967 Vic Elford and David Stone won the Corsica Rally in a 911R prototype – in accordance with the Porsche motto that development moves quickest in motor sports.

A Porsche 911R during testing at the famous Mont Ventoux in southern France, 1967. 210 hp and a weight of just 820 kilos made for a lively ride.

26_ Porsche 917

From a Beast to a Cult Item

No Porsche is as fascinating as the 917. This racing car resulted from a revolution at Porsche, led by Ferdinand Piëch. In 1963 Ferry Porsche's nephew joined the company. In 1965 he took over development and motor sports, and brought a vision with him: to make Porsche the endurance world champion and overall winner in Le Mans. Watched with suspicion by Ferry and the family, Piëch ordered an eye-wateringly expensive and awe-inspiringly fast racer for the 1969 season: the 917 with a brand-new 4.5-litre twelve-cylinder engine and, initially, 580 horsepower.

This car is at the centre of countless stories of far too much power and far too little handling at first, of courage and recklessness, and finally of crushing superiority. Of the earliest test drives, plagued by aquaplaning and side winds, ending with a completely wrecked 917 but a miraculously unharmed driver. Of the drivers refusing to take this wild animal out on the Nürburgring in 1969. Of Hans Herrmann and Richard Attwood 1970 driving the over-powered beast to its first Le Mans victory in torrential rain. Of the British driver Derek Bell reaching 396 km/h in tests at Le Mans in 1971. Of Helmut Marko and Gijs van Lennep winning the race at a record average speed of 222 km/h. This record stood for 39 years. In the world championship the 917 put every competitor to the slaughter – in 1970 and 1971 Porsche was practically invincible. And then a rule change put an end to these triumphs.

Yet the 917 had unlimited potential. Porsche adapted it for races in the USA and fitted the car with turbo engines, then a revolutionary innovation. With up to 1,300 hp the 917 won the CanAm championships in 1972 and 1973. What had happened in the world championship was then repeated: in order to end the dominance of the 917, the rule book was rewritten. This Porsche could only be beaten in a committee room.

___ The 24 Hours of Le Mans in 1971: the short-tail 917 of the Martini Racing Team in the pits. This car won the race at a record average speed of 222 km/h.

27__ Porsche 911 Carrera RS 2.7

The Revolutionary

In the early 1970s the 911, accustomed to victory, was under pressure on race tracks. The upstart Ford Capri and BMW CSL were whizzing across the line ahead of the Porsche. A remedy was needed: a 911 for the road that was also a basis for motor sports. Porsche boss Ernst Fuhrmann gave the go-ahead for a revolutionary, the 911 Carrera RS 2.7.

The RS 2.7 was different from any 911 before it. It had the "ducktail": a rear spoiler for greater stability and for downforce on fast corners. It had tyres with different widths at the front and back (which the sales and service teams thought was lunacy). It had Nikasil cylinder lining for high rpm. The 2.7-litre boxer engine generated 210 hp at 6,300 revolutions. Now that is quite something, but the royally dimensioned disk brakes (282.5 mm at the front, 300 mm at the back) had a bitingly effective answer. The RS 2.7 didn't hang around: 100 km/h after 5.8 seconds, a top speed of 245 km/h. The RS 2.7 was the first 911 to be honoured as a "Carrera", a name not used since the 356. Its dynamism encouraged the occupants' sporting spirit. Comfort? Forget it. Well, the Touring version pampers them with adjustable seats, a radio, a glove compartment cover and handles for closing the doors. Decadent accessories like that, absent on the Sport model, give the Touring a weight of 1,075 kilograms, while the Sport version weighs 960 kilos and costs 34,000 deutschmarks.

The sales team are muttering: a 911 with a spoiler? No comfort? As noisy as a sawmill? 10,000 marks more than the S Class? You can't sell that! On the contrary: when it was presented at the Paris Autosalon in October 1972, Porsche sold 55 of the Carrera RS 2.7. Six weeks later the whole planned production of 500 was sold out. After an amazing 1,580 of the RS 2.7, Porsche stopped making them. In late 2015, well-preserved examples were selling for almost one million euros.

___ A pure driving machine: the 911 Carrera RS 2.7 was the most radical 911 to be made in quantity. Today this stripped-down Porsche is rare and valuable.

Advertising photos of the 1970s should tell a story. This one might be: "Darling, no outing this Sunday. I've fallen in love with racing in the RS 2.7."

28__ 911 Carrera RSR 2.1 Turbo

The First One with a Charger

So which was the first 911 Turbo? Okay, at the IAA in 1973 there was a concept car that Porsche used to explore whether there was interest in a super sports car at the time of the "oil crisis". Leaving out this exhibition piece, the first 911 Turbo that snarled in public was the 911 Carrera RSR Turbo 2.1. This was on 24 March 1974, when this racing car with the massive rear end did laps of the Circuit de la Sarthe in practice for the 24 Hours of Le Mans.

Porsche put its faith in turbocharging because in US motor sports the company had already gained a wealth of experience with and earned laurels for this technology, which was new for racing cars. The newly developed 6-cylinder boxer engine, with 2.1 litres capacity, a turbocharger and intercooler, generated a good 500 hp. In order to make the car light, the artists in Weissach took out their metal cutters and removed from the raw bodywork of a 911 everything that could legally be removed. The doors, bonnet and wings consisted of paper-thin plastic, the roll-over bar of aluminium, the seat rails of titanium. The space given to the back seats in a civilian 911 was devoted to the 120-litre tank in the RSR Turbo. Thanks to this unorthodox position, the handling remained reasonably constant as the tank emptied. The massive wheels and brakes came from the legendary Porsche 917. The whole car weighed 825 kilograms and went from nought to 200 km/h in 8.8 seconds.

The most important event in 1974 was Le Mans, of course, where the RSR Turbo, the first racing car to compete with a turbocharger, sensationally took second place against prototypes that were much lighter. Porsche could have won the race, as the Matra that was in the lead had gear problems. Instead the Porsche mechanics repaired their competitor's gear box, and the Matra won. The reason for this was that Porsche had developed the 'box for the French team.

___ The large wing created downforce and served as a housing for the intercooler.

_____ This view (far left) at a
corner in Le Mans reveals
the turbocharger in the rear
of the 911. The large rear
wing kept the Porsche on
course through fast bends
and on long straights.

29__ Porsche 911 Turbo 3.0

The Most Anticyclical Porsche in History

In 1973 the oil exporters turned off the taps, and the price quadrupled within a year. Bankruptcy and short-time working on all sides, car-free Sundays and speed limits. In the middle of this downbeat mood, Porsche burst in with the 911 Turbo. In autumn 1974 the most anticyclical Porsche ever graced the motor show in Paris. It was the Swabian answer to the Italian twelve-cylinder wonders. As this answer could not be given with the three-litre suction engine of the 911, in avant-garde style Porsche turned to the turbocharger. In 1972 the team had demoralised its competitors in American motor sports with charged-up engines, and now had incomparable knowledge of turbo technology.

With a turbo-charger, the three-litre engine of the "Type 930", as this road racer was called internally, produced 260 horsepower. This catapulted the 1,195 kilogram rear-engine machine to 100 km/h in 5.5 seconds. It maxed out at 250 km/h. Wider wings, a rear wing and a front spoiler, as well as generously sized tyres, 185 at the front and 215 at the back, underlined Porsche's message: this is the fastest sports car that you can buy in Germany. On two conditions – firstly, you have 65,800 deutschmarks to spare; and secondly, you are not easily scared. When you put your foot on the gas pedal, with a slight delay ("the turbo gap") you get a massive shove from behind ("the turbo kick"), and the car goes off like a missile.

The Porsche racing driver Jürgen Barth and the journalist Gustav Büsing put it like this in the *Big Book of Porsche Types*: "The driver who wanted to exploit to the full the capabilities of the drivetrain in combination with the engine performance had ... to possess above-average driving ability." Just so, but you could enjoy the fright of the 911 Turbo in style, as Porsche crammed every imaginable luxury into this road racer. And it paid off: the 911 Turbo became the company flagship.

___ Germany's fastest sports car of the day in action. With 260 hp, the 911 Turbo rocketed from zero to 100 km/h in 5.5 seconds.

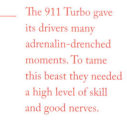 The 911 Turbo gave its drivers many adrenalin-drenched moments. To tame this beast they needed a high level of skill and good nerves.

30__ Porsche 928

Too Far Ahead of Its Time

In 1971 it seemed clear that a more modern sports car was needed to replace the 911. Chairman of the board Ernst Fuhrmann, together with the Porsche and Piëch families, saw that the end was coming for the 911. The rear-engine design and the six-cylinder boxer engine seemed antiquated. Air-cooled and noisy, unsuitable for progressive technology such as four-valve cylinder heads, the engine would soon fail to comply with noise and emissions regulations in important markets. Its successor, with the development number 928, was therefore fitted with a highly modern, flat-built V8. Water-cooled, made of light alloy, and large enough to make even Americans happy.

The V8 was at the front, and its power was transmitted to the gearbox on the rear axle via a shaft. This principle, called "transaxle", results in an excellent distribution of weight. The specially devised "Weissach" rear axle irons out even serious driving errors and keeps the back end stable. A light-alloy chassis, aluminium bonnet and boot covers, nose and tail made from malleable plastic, lots of luggage space and a bodywork design that was ahead of its time. This adds up to a superb sports car. Over the next two decades the 928 got better, more powerful and faster. When it was presented in 1977, its 4.5-litre V8 generated 240 horsepower; the last 928 GTS in 1992 had a 5.4-litre whopper with a four-valve head and 350 hp under the bonnet.

Nevertheless: the 928 was no 911. Die-hard Porsche fans gave it the cold shoulder. And this remained the case throughout its life. From 1977 to 1995 Porsche made 61,056 of the Gran Turismo. By way of comparison: the third generation of the 911 reached approximately the same quantity (63,700) in only five years of production between 1989 and 1993. It is only now that connoisseurs are discovering their love of the avant-garde design and robust technology of the rare 928.

____ Advertising from the 1970s: a pipe-smoking Porsche driver and a lady whose choice of coat today matches the colour of the car.

31__ Type 953

Four-Wheel Drive for the Sahara

Four-wheel drive for the 911. A feature that went into series production in 1986 with the 959 super sports car and in 1988 with the 911 Carrera 4 was first tested by Porsche in motor sports. It was like this: the racing driver Jacky Ickx had won the Paris–Dakar Rally in a Mercedes in 1983 and suggested to Helmuth Bott, Porsche's head of technology, that Porsche could do the same in 1984 with a 911. Bott summoned his head of racing, Peter Falk, and the engineer Roland Kussmaul: "Can we compete in the 1984 Dakar?" Falk and Kussmaul nodded: "Yes, but please can we have your company car for testing?" Bott took a deep breath and gave them his 911, which Kussmaul had already converted to 4WD using Audi parts, as Porsche was researching in this field. 30 per cent of the power went to the front, 70 per cent to the rear axle.

For the desert, at the front the engineer installed double transverse control arms and two shock absorbers on each side, at the back a reinforced axle from the 911 Turbo. Two fuel tanks had a combined capacity of 270 litres. A welded-in steel cage took care of safety. The 3.2-litre engine produced the standard 225 horsepower. In late summer 1983 Kussmaul, Falk and two colleagues thrashed this "Type 953" around an army training ground in Lower Saxony, day and night for a weekend, driving 1,500 kilometres. That was risky, as here – unlike in the desert – trees stood close to the route. And the car was doing 210 km/h.

In September 1983 the team went to the Sahara, where the grand-daddy of all 4WD 911s covered 5,000 kilometres more. Porsche made three 911 Carrera 4x4s modelled on the 953 and tackled the company's first Paris-to-Dakar ordeal ordeal in January 1984. The French driver René Metge brought victory home to Zuffenhausen. It was the first-ever win for a sports car over the 11,000 kilometres of torture. And Ickx? And the first 953? Ickx came in sixth, and the gallant 953 met its destiny in the metal press.

____ Autumn 1983 in the depths of the Sahara: a short service stop for the board member's 911, which was hammered through 5,000 kilometres of desert as a 4WD-test mule.

___ Winter 1983 saw the last test
drives with the Type 953,
which was to compete in and win
the Paris–Dakar Rally in 1984
as a 911 Carrera 3.2 4x4.

32_ Porsche Cayenne

An Offroad Milestone

The Cayenne gets round the north loop of the Nürburgring faster than most sports cars. And definitely faster than any other sports utility vehicle. This is the status in spring 2016: the time is 7 minutes, 59.74 seconds. Offroad, too, the Cayenne is one of the best. It survives 10,000 kilometres at a brisk pace from Berlin to Lake Baikal without complaint – this was the news for fans after the Transsyberia Rally in 2006, 2007 and 2008 (in the last two years the route was from Moscow to Ulan-Bator). So much on the subject of "sports".

There is also something to be said about "utility". A Cayenne is spacious, a fantastic car for travelling. It pulls any horse box from the stables at escape velocity, and is superb for driving up to the opera house (the recent generations, at least). However, the decisive point seems to be that, whether for sports or utility, the Porsche name stands for sports-car engineering, here spiced with a sprinkling of pepper from the harbour town on Devil's Island. Today Porsche makes the Cayenne with a diesel engine, with hybrid power, with a "small" V6 or a powerful V8 engine.

The Cayenne was controversial at Porsche, when an SUV came under consideration: a utility vehicle from Porsche? The last time this was tried, and failed, was the late 1950s. And a giant SUV fits the model range the way a bodybuilder fits into the Stuttgart ballet ensemble. At 2.2 tonnes and up to 570 horsepower, it is still a matter of public controversy, especially when the subject of climate change is discussed.

For all that, the Cayenne has been a huge success for Porsche. Shortly after presentation of this third series of models, alongside the 911 and Boxster, in September 2002, the sales figures rocketed. In 2015 the Cayenne, at around 73,000 units, accounted for a third of all Porsches sold.

___ Yes, the Cayenne is extremely well equipped for off-road trips. However, very few Porsche owners subject their high-end SUV to such an ordeal.

Umberto Maglioli, waiting for the start of the Targa Florio in 1956 in a 550 A Spyder. He was to win this road race in Sicily after almost eight hours behind the wheel.

RACING DRIVERS

33__ Hans Herrmann

Historic Victories, a Wise Retirement

"It's not perfect as it is, but you could just about leave it like that." The mechanics were relieved to hear these words, spoken by Hans Herrmann after hours-long attempts to adjust his seat. This Swabian driver, born on 23 February 1928 and at Porsche since 1953, was notorious for his demands regarding the seat of a racing car. He was admired for his skills as a test driver – and as a man who achieved historic successes in 130 races for Porsche.

In 1954 he took a little 550 Spyder to third place in the Carrera Panamericana through Mexico, thus announcing the arrival of Porsche in the symphony of great marques. In 1958 Herrmann and Jean Behra drove a 718 RSK to third place in Le Mans – the first time Porsche drivers climbed the podium at the world's most famous endurance race. In 1960 the team of Herrmann and Gendebien won the 12 Hours of Sebring for Porsche for the first time. 1970 was the year of his *finale furioso*: in a 580-hp 917, Herrmann and Richard Attwood gained the coveted overall victory for Porsche at Le Mans. The rain lashed down, and only seven cars out of 51 made it into the classification.

Herrmann was 42 years old and then announced his retirement, as he had promised his wife Magdalena before the race. Perhaps Herrmann himself thought he had challenged fate often enough, especially when he raced for other marques in Formula 1. When he crashed into a wall and broke several bones driving a Mercedes in practice for the 1955 Monaco Grand Prix. When his brakes failed at the Avus in Berlin in the BRM Formula 1 in 1959 at 280 km/h, he was thrown from the car and escaped with scratches. But also in 1954, when he shot beneath an almost closed railway barrier with Herbert Linge in a Porsche 550 at the Mille Miglia. They called him "Lucky Hans". Every man is the architect of his own fortune, as they say, and Herrmann confirmed this with his wise retirement.

___ Many highlights in the history of Porsche motor sports are associated with the name Hans Herrmann. With Richard Attwood he gained the marque's first victory at Le Mans.

34__ Herbert Linge

"That ain't fast!"

This is the crisp reply that Peter Falk received from Herbert Linge when he asked the master mechanic, test driver and racing driver to take it easy with the 911 when conditions were slippery at the Monte Carlo Rally in 1965. Falk, later head of sports at Porsche, was Linge's co-driver. The man at the wheel kept his foot down, and the pair finished fifth in the rally.

Herbert Linge, born in Weissach on 11 June 1928, was one of the all-rounders who made his mark on Porsche in the early years. In 1943 he began an apprenticeship as a mechanic and was the first fitter that Porsche re-employed after the war. Linge quickly rose to head the workshop, brought customer service in the USA up to scratch, and in 1959 showed Ferdinand Porsche a field in the commune of Weissach: the future site of Porsche's think-tank. His racing career began by chance: "I had experience of racing motorbikes. When no one else had time, they asked me if I wanted to drive one of the cars." He did, and he could. 89 victories all around the world and four world championship titles are the statistics of this Swabian veteran. Who knows how many wins he would have chalked up if it had not been for Le Mans in 1969. Linge was going to drive a 917 along with the private British driver John Woolfe. Immediately after the start Woolfe had a fatal crash – and Linge withdrew from racing. He only returned to Le Mans once, in order to take part in Steve McQueen's "Le Mans" epic in 1970.

In the early 1970s Linge invented the emergency service for race tracks that could get to a crashed driver within 60 seconds. In 1982 he was awarded the Bundesverdienstkreuz, Germany's top civilian honour, for this. In the late 1980s Linge originated the Carrera Cup, a series of races that is now held worldwide. In 1992 it was time to shift down to a lower gear, and Linge retired.

____ Herbert Linge was a legendary all-rounder at Porsche: master mechanic, responsible for service in the USA, racing and rally driver, and originator of a race series.

35__ Vic Elford

Two Premieres and an Impossible Win

"Once, after completing a special stage, it took me three attempts to light my cigarette," said Vic Elford to reporters on 26 January 1968. This is a remarkable statement. Firstly, it comes from a genius at the wheel, who had just defeated the rest of the world's elite in a 911 T with 180 hp on ice, snow and asphalt, gaining Porsche's first overall victory in the Monte Carlo Rally. Secondly, this British driver was a dedicated chain smoker whose handling of a cigarette lighter was immaculate.

Two days later, Elford was sitting in a Boeing 707, heading for Daytona in Florida. Three works-entered 907s started the 24-hour race. Elford switched from a 911 weighing a ton with a rear engine to a 600-kilogram lightweight, a Type 907. The 270 hp of its 2.2-litre mid-engine produced a top speed of 325 km/h. The Daytona Speedway is a combination of steep-banked curves at full throttle and fiddly in-field driving. In the night one of the factory Porsches overturned and slid across the course on its roof, spraying sparks. Elford was right behind it: "I hurtled blindly into a chaos of smoke and dust, and emerged on the other side without hitting anything." On 4 February Elford and his team mate Rolf Stommelen crossed the line as winners. It was the first overall victory for Porsche in a major endurance race.

At the Targa Florio on 5 May, he surpassed even that. The Sicilian road race is held over ten laps, each 71.9 kilo-metres with around 700 bends. On the first lap, Elford's 907 lost a wheel twice: 18 minutes lost to the leader. He attacked, then handed over briefly to his team mate Umberto Maglioli. On the last three laps Elford produced pyrotechnic driving, setting two new records and achieving a win that had seemed impossible. For the first time, on the traditional "victory poster", Porsche depicted not a car, but a driver: Vic Elford.

___ Until Elford's triumph in the Targa Florio in 1968, the victory posters showed Porsche racing cars. A portrait was a novelty – and homage to the British driver.

TARGA
FLORIO

36__Joseph Siffert

Speed in His Blood

The 1,000-kilometre race on the Nürburgring in 1968. Jo Siffert and Vic Elford are driving a works-team 908. The weekend starts badly, with their eight-cylinder engine playing up in practice: they start in 27th place! At the start in Le Mans style, the drivers sprint to their waiting cars and rocket away. Siffert runs faster than anyone else, and shoots off as if propelled by a catapult. At the braking point for the first corner, he is lying third. At the end of the first lap, his white Porsche is the leader. Elford and Siffert win, the second victory for Porsche in the leading German sports-car race.

A few weeks later Siffert put in the best practice time in Le Mans. Never before had a Porsche started from pole position there. No doubt about it: he was the fastest man in the team. In 1969 it got even better. Swiss Jo, also known as "Seppi", together with the British driver Brian Redman, won Porsche's first world championship, and came in first at the end of the season in the Austrian Grand Prix in a Porsche 917. It was the first victory for the twelve-cylinder racer, which was extremely tricky to drive. "We loved Jo Siffert": Siffert's relationship to the Porsche team was succinctly described by Peter Falk, head of racing. Then Ferrari put out feelers to Siffert, talking about Formula 1 and sports cars. Porsche had to prevent this, and offered to help their fastest man find his way into a Formula 1 cockpit. Siffert decided in favour of March, and Porsche provided 30,000 US dollars to support development of the 701 Monoposto.

In 1970 Siffert had a tough competitor in the Porsche: the Mexican Pedro Rodriguez was often faster than Jo. These two alpha males fought out legendary battles such as the 1,000-kilometre race in Spa in 1971. That same year Siffert met the tragic fate of many of his colleagues: he crashed fatally in a Formula 1 race.

___ The Swiss driver Jo Siffert was long regarded as the fastest man in the Porsche works team. With his colleague Brian Redman he gained Porsche's first world championship in 1969.

37__ Gerhard Mitter

European Champion with a Foot in Plaster

Gerhard Mitter, born in 1935, was a Swabian from Leonberg and a universal genius of his day at driving. When he came to Porsche in 1964, Mitter already had a reputation as an engine tuner and an excellent racing driver with Grand Prix experience. He was suspicious, marking his racing cars in secret places so that no one could give him a different car without his knowledge. On the other hand Mitter was also a really good guy, who invited the team to his home near Leonberg and roasted a sucking pig for them.

Mitter drove everything: 24 hours, 1,000-kilometre races, the Targa Florio (790 kilometres, around 8,000 bends), which he won in 1969 with Udo Schütz. But he was at his best in sprints. In 1966, 1967 and 1968 he was European hill climb champion: sprint races of six to 21 kilometres on closed roads. Hill climb specials like the Porsche 910/8 and 909 were ultra-light racers with engines tuned to squeeze out the very last drop. Next to the road were precipices on one side, rock walls on the other, and for relaxation in-between tens of thousands of spectators with their toes at the roadside. None of which bothered Mitter, who was as hard as nails. In 1966 he smashed into a wall of rock at a race in Spa and broke his left foot. This did not stop him from competing. The plaster on his foot would have crumbled on the hard clutch pedal, so for the next race Mitter had it wrapped in plastic. The material gets very hot when it hardens out, but Mitter bore it without complaint – and became European champion.

After overturning in a world championship race in Daytona, his Porsche thundered past the pits upside down on the roll-over bar, in a stream of sparks. Mitter later told the horrified Porsche team: "I could easily have lit a cigarette on the glowing bar." On 1 August 1969, in a BMW Formula 2 on the Nürburgring, the dauntless Mitter suffered a fatal crash.

____ Fast, self-confident, technically competent and tough: Gerhard Mitter. In 1966 he won the European mountain-racing championship with a foot in plaster.

38_ Hurley Haywood

America's Best Endurance Racer

How do you become America's most successful endurance racing driver? The best way to do it is to compete at autocross in a noisy Corvette as a 20-year-old student in Florida and win against a famous driver like Peter Gregg. Ideally, this Peter Gregg just happens to be a Porsche dealer and owns a racing team like Brumos.

And this is exactly how Hurley Haywood's career started in 1968. The story continued as follows: Gregg, eight years older, helped Haywood to buy a racing car and showed him a few tricks. After a day's training the student left his teacher behind once again. This was the beginning of a friendship, and it was surely a positive that the two of them had the same birthday: 4 May. For the 6-hour race at Watkins Glen on 12 July 1969, the two of them took turns at the wheel of a racing car for the first time. It was a 911 S, and they won in their category. In 1973 Haywood and Gregg sensationally won the 24 Hours of Daytona in a Carrera RSR 2.8, and the incomparable career of Hurley Haywood over long distances took off. He won the big classic races ten times: Daytona five times (1973, 1975, 1977, 1979, 1991), Le Mans three times (1977, 1983, 1994) and Sebring twice (1974, 1981). In a Porsche every time, always starting with number 59. Haywood amassed eight national titles, and even the man himself probably does not know how many Halls of Fame honour him. The Motorsports Hall of Fame of America is certainly one of them.

In 2009, at the tender age of 60, Haywood took the winners' podium in Daytona for the last time: he had come in third in a Brumos prototype with a four-litre Porsche engine. And first place also went to a Brumos. Which greatly pleased Haywood, because since Peter Gregg's early death in 1980 he had attended closely to both the car dealership and the racing team that bore the old-established name of Brumos.

___ Hurley Haywood in the cockpit of a Porsche 917/10 in 1973. The most successful American endurance driver took the winners' podium for the last time in 2009, at the age of 60.

39__Jacky Ickx

Thoughtfully Fast

Jacky Ickx, born in Brussels in 1945, was one of the world's fastest racing drivers, but sometimes he demanded patience. Especially when reporters wanted a quick answer. "Come back tomorrow – I have to think about your questions." He made his reputation as a young man at Formula 1 with Ferrari and at endurance racing with Ford and others.

In 1969 Ickx made headlines at Le Mans, boycotting the famous start, when the drivers ran across the track to their cars. They fastened their seat belts later on the long straight at over 300 km/h, holding the steering wheel between their knees. Ickx strolled across the track, calmly fastened his belt, set off in last position, and won the race after a duel with the Porsche 908 driven by Hans Herrmann. Between 1976 and 1985 Ickx was a regular in Porsches entered by the factory. The team members with whom he won Le Mans four times (1976, 1977, 1981, 1982) and became endurance world champion twice (1982, 1983) still enthuse about his intelligence, his concentration on victory, his spurning of superficial show, and his speed. Stories of how he chased the front-runners in darkness and foul weather are told with a pleasurable shudder: how he thrashed a 936 from 42nd place into the lead on a rainy night in Le Mans in 1977, how three years later he drove the 908/80 from nowhere to the front of the field.

Away from the track and off-road, Ickx discovered the Sahara, won the Paris–Dakar Rally in 1983 in a Mercedes, and encouraged Porsche to start up a desert programme. His sixth place in a 911 in 1984 would have been unremarkable if Ickx had not driven to the finish from 139th position undeterred by a cable that caught fire. Not to mention his second place in 1986. Or the occasion in 2015, when the author asked him a question, and he replied: "Come back tomorrow…"

___ Four wins at Le Mans, two endurance world championships. Jacky Ickx is a fast, highly eloquent man. The only word he doesn't know is "give up".

40__David Piper

Madly in Love with the 917

David Piper was born to a British farming family in 1930. The Pipers were so well off that their son could devote himself from an early age to buying racing cars and testing their limits. Rico Steinemann, the head of racing at Porsche, knew that "Pipes" had a talent for this. In May 1969, Steinemann dialled Piper's number and asked if he would like to drive a new Porsche. The background to this was that the works-team drivers flatly refused to take out the new Type 917 for the 1,000-kilometre race at the Nürburgring. 580 horsepower, 380 km/h top speed and scant road-holding were frightening even for these hard-bitten guys.

Piper and the Australian racing driver Frank Gardner travelled to the Nürburgring. "The fast stretches were terrible, it was hardly possible to control the car", Piper later reminisced. But the two of them held on, took eighth place and gave the 917 its first racing result. After this, Piper's next step was unavoidable: he bought a 917 and entered the 1,000-kilometre race in Buenos Aires in 1970, marking the first appearance of the 917 in the Americas. On the voyage back to Europe, the freighter carrying the Porsche stopped in Miami, where Piper's friends Peter Gregg and Tony Dean took the car ashore without further ado to compete in the 24 Hours of Daytona in January. Piper had no idea about this, but he attended the race: "Then I saw my Porsche whistling round the banked corners." To top it all, Gregg and Dean ruined the engine, "and eventually paid me 300 dollars".

Piper's liaison with the 917 did not end there, but took a dramatic turn. Driving as a stuntman in 1970 while Steve McQueen's "Le Mans" was being filmed, he had a serious crash in a 917 – part of one leg had to be amputated. His career was over, but his love of racing cars still burned. At the age of well over 80, the gentleman racer was still to be seen at tracks all over the world.

___ David Piper was one of the first to drive the fearsome Porsche 917 in racing, and later played a part in the film "Le Mans" as a stuntman.

41__Derek Bell

Nothing But Racing

He is an excellent racing driver, and he looks the part. Born in 1941 in England, and never officially retired from the sport, Derek Bell moves elegantly and nimbly at the Porsche Racing Reunion in 2015, a wonderful celebration of motor-sport nostalgia in California, with a charming and quick-witted manner of chatting. He is wiry, his angular face with an aquiline nose looks aristocratic, and his long, straight hair conveys nonchalance. And when he eases into the cockpit of a 1980s Porsche 962C, the flow of his movements shows that he has done this a hundred times – and that he still enjoys it.

In the late 1960s, Bell drove single-seaters for Ferrari, but his talent did not truly blossom between free-standing wheels. Racing sports cars was a different matter altogether. In 1970 he gained a place without difficulty in the famous JWA team, which ran the 917 über-cars for Porsche. In 1975, with JWA though in an English car, he won in Le Mans for the first time. Over two decades, Bell drove for Porsche again and again, and he was a winner. Le Mans in 1981, 1982, 1986 and 1987. Twice with Jacky Ickx, twice with Hans-Joachim Stuck. In 1985 and 1986 he was sports-car world champion driving a Porsche. In his book "24:16", the engineer Norbert Singer enthused about Bell's clear statements as a test driver and his sensitivity for racing cars – how he took his foot off the accelerator very briefly on the six-kilometre-long straight in Le Mans in order to give the engine a moment's respite, or how he nudged the brake with his left foot at the end of the Mulsanne-straight in order to warm it for the brutal deceleration that was to follow.

Even when Bell's days in the works-team cockpit were over, he could not give up. In 1995 at Le Mans he drove a McLaren with his son Justin (born in 1968) to a sensational third place. And this time Bell called it a day.

____ Fast, reliable, a superb team player: Derek Bell became endurance world champion twice with Porsche. This photo was taken in 1971.

42__Hans-Joachim Stuck

From the Zugspitze

12 June 1985, practice for the 24-hour race in Le Mans. Hans-Joachim Stuck is 34 years old. He has already had a great career racing touring cars, and less happy times in Formula 1. In December 1984 Stuck came to Porsche, and now he drives the 962C for the works team. This is his chance to make a comeback, and Stuck takes it.

The car's turbo engine generates 700 horsepower. Thanks to ingenious aerodynamics it is glued to the road, permitting crazy speeds through the corners. A lap is 13.6 kilometres long, and the stop-watch records 3:14.80 minutes, an average speed of 251.815 km/h. No one has ever driven so fast in Le Mans, and until 2016 no one will be so fast again (though admittedly the course became slower after rebuilding). The Bavarian Stuck didn't win the race, but with his team colleague Derek Bell he became endurance world champion in 1985. The victory at Le Mans finally came in 1986, and was repeated in 1987. Stuck was gloriously successful, and sometimes played the entertainer for his team. In 1986, when the Queen made Derek Bell a Member of the Most Excellent Order of the British Empire (MBE), Bell's mechanics adorned his Porsche with the letters "MBE". Stuck's head of racing, Peter Falk, recalls that "When Stuck saw that, he said to us: ›And what goes on my car?‹ Then he proposed: ›V.d.Z.‹ We gave him a puzzled look, and he explained: ›Von der Zugspitze‹." (Germany's highest mountain, in Bavaria).

Following a stint at Audi, Stuck stayed with Porsche until the nineties, raced in the USA, and delighted the fans there by yodelling via the track sound system. In 2011, in an emotional farewell to the cockpit, Stuck drove the 24-hour race on the Nürburgring with his two sons. Since 2012 he has been an active president of the German Motorsports Federation who charms those around him with his cleverness and wit.

___ To this day no one has driven a faster lap than Hans-Joachim Stuck on the high-speed course at Le Mans. His average speed in 1985 was 251.8 km/h.

43__ René Metge

The Friendly Desert King

The Paris–Dakar Rally in 1984, at dead of night, in a camp at the end of an 800-kilometre day's run. It is bitterly cold in the Sahara as one by one the cars emerge from the desert, some of them in a dire state, the drivers and co-drivers exhausted and burned out. Then the works-team Porsche 911 Carrera 4x4 rolls up. The cap-wearing driver, René Metge, releases his safety belt, climbs out of the low bucket seat behind the steering wheel, gives a friendly greeting to all around, and contentedly lights a Gauloise. Then he walks off, clearly in an extremely good mood and fit as a fiddle. Everyone in the camp waves to the French driver.

Metge, born in 1941, loved the rally, and everyone loved Metge. Porsche had a special affection for him, as he and his co-driver Dominique Lemoyne won the 1984 Paris-Dakar, the very first time it was attempted in a 911. This was an incredible achievement for the team and the technology, as hitherto only all-terrain vehicles had been able to win this marathon event – a 12,000-kilometre-long torture session held for the first time in 1977. And there is no doubt that most of the credit for this success is due to Metge. Few people knew the desert as he did, and he knew what his car could stand. Metge helped Porsche to organise this first entry by the Stuttgart company; he knew the people who mattered in every oasis and was a friend of the organiser, Thierry Sabine. In 1985 Metge was almost victorious again, but a ruptured oil pipe put paid to his hopes. In 1986 he returned and won once more, this time in a Porsche 959. It was one of the toughest versions of the Dakar rally: 13,800 kilometres. Of the 280 cars that set off, no more than 31 reached the finish in the West African town of Dakar.

As for the cap: Metge was never seen without his veteran headgear – neither in the camp, nor in the car, nor even in his sleeping bag. Everyone agreed that they would not recognise René without his cap. Except perhaps by his laugh and the Gauloise.

____ René Metge (right) and his co-driver Dominique Lemoyne were celebrating even before the start of the 1984 Paris–Dakar Rally. This was prophetic: they won.

44_ Bob Wollek

The Unfulfilled Dream of Le Mans

Bob Wollek from Alsace was one of the most successful Porsche racing drivers. He seldom drove a works car, but over a 25-year period from the 1970s private teams repeatedly contracted this quiet man with economical body language. Wollek was the only seven-times winner of the Porsche Cup, an annual award given by Porsche from 1970 for the most successful private racing driver.

Wollek had speed in his blood. Born in 1943, in the mid-1960s he was one of the fastest French skiers, winning three gold and two silver medals at the university winter games between 1966 and 1968. Following an accident while training for the Winter Olympics, he switched to racing cars, and carried on winning. "Brilliant Bob" was fast in any car, and he loved driving a Porsche. He was as assured in the bear-like 935 as he was in the 956 and 962, whose cornering speeds frightened some drivers to death. In 1982 and 1983 Wollek was the German champion racing driver. In the 962 he won the 24 Hours of Daytona four times. Wollek was famous for his sensitive treatment of his cars, and nobody could ever understand how he managed to consume so little fuel.

Yet he never climbed to the summit of his personal ambitions: the 24-Hours of Le Mans. Wollek entered 30 times between 1968 and 2000. Sometimes he came close to making his dream come true – always in a Porsche. In 1978, 1995 and 1996 he was runner-up, in 1981 he took third place. In 1997 Wollek was in the lead when the rear of his 911 GT1 hit something after a skid, and the transmission shaft broke. After this the mechanics led him through the drivers' camp looking like a seriously ill man. A year later he took second place. On 16 March 2001 Bob Wollek was riding a bicycle from his hotel to the Sebring International Raceway. At 57, this was how he kept fit. A campervan hit him from behind, and Wollek died at the site of the accident.

_____ Bob Wollek won medals as a skier and was successful in racing cars. But in 30 starts at Le Mans, his pursuit of victory was in vain.

45__ Walter Röhrl

Drive Flawlessly, Speak Frankly

Porsche and Walter Röhrl belong together. But wait a moment: he was world rally champion in 1980 with Fiat and in 1982 with Opel. In 1983 he could easily have done it with Lancia, but there was too much circus for his taste. Then Röhrl made rally history with Audi: Quattro! S1! A 550-hp driving machine with an early four-wheel drive that could only be mastered with the instincts and reflexes of a god. His trademark, alongside a mastery of cars that was out of this world: he was a nonconformist to the marrow. Advertising events for the main sponsor? "Pooh, I was hired as a driver, not an actor." And he was honest, whatever the cost: a wonderful contract with Mercedes for 1981 was never signed because he explained to the board that they wouldn't win so much as a coconut with the 500 SL as it then was.

And Porsche? Porsche was Röhrl's first love, and it was requited in a strange manner. In 1967 Röhrl was 20, secretary and driver to the finance director of the bishopric of Regensburg. His brother had told him: "Buy a Porsche. It's the only decent car." So Walter saved up and bought a 356 with no engine. Luckily his brother had a four-cylinder engine in the garage. From 1968 Röhrl drove in rallies, competing again and again in a Porsche that friends prepared for him – including friends at Porsche such as Jürgen Barth and Roland Kussmaul. In 1981 they prepared a 911 in which Röhrl came within a whisker of beating the all-conquering Audi Quattro in a world championship event in Italy. Occasionally Röhrl helped out at Porsche as a test driver, and in the early 1980s drove one of the first 4WD 911s with development boss Helmuth Bott. After years at Audi, in late 1992 Walter Röhrl signed a contract with Porsche: development driver and ambassador for the brand. In this role, too, he remained true to himself: drive flawlessly, speak frankly.

____ Porsche was Walter Röhrl's first love. Twice world rally champion, he has been wedded to the marque since late 1992 – and it is still a happy marriage.

You had to be brave to drive this machine. The 917 PA Spyder of 1969 weighed a mere 775 kilograms and was accelerated very rapidly indeed by the 4.5-litre, twelve-cylinder engine with 580 hp.

EXTREMISTS

46__Porsche 909 Mountain Spyder

Extreme climber

The date is 22 September 1968 in the small French town of Bédoin at the foot of Mont Ventoux. Vineyards lie all around. Grey-coated Porsche technicians are pushing a tiny racing car into their Opel Blitz transporter. The 909 Mountain Spyder has not won the final of the European hill-climbing championships, the famous 21.6-kilometre sprint up to the meteorological station – this feat was achieved by Gerhard Mitter in an older, tried-and-tested 910/8 mountain racer, ensuring that Porsche won its ninth European title since 1958. But the 909 Mountain Spyder, just under 3.45 metres long, 1.80 metres wide and 71 centimetres high, put in a nutshell the future of motor sports at Porsche.

Firstly, at 384 kilograms this Lilliputian car was an extreme case study in the art of light-weight construction. The titanium suspension, the frame of thin aluminium tubes, the beryllium brake disks, the silver wiring, paper-thin bodywork and completely pared-down engine – all of this already existed in the 910/8. But the 909 went further. It had no fuel pump. Instead 15 litres of petrol sloshed about in a titanium ball. Before the start, a mechanic pressurised the fuel with nitrogen, and the pressure conveyed it for injection. Secondly, the 909 had excellent weight distribution, as the driver, engine and gearbox had been shifted a long way to the front. To make this trick possible, the limited-slip differential was placed behind the five-gear box. Thanks to this ingenious balance, the 909 went round corners like a weasel.

This configuration showed the way ahead for later Porsche legends like the 908/03, but from the drivers it demanded absolute faith in the kindness of fate and their own abilities: they now squatted just behind the front axle, their legs projecting into the spindly web of the tube frame. All of this with a 275-hp, eight-cylinder engine at their back that powered the 909 from zero to 100 in 2.5 seconds.

____ The 909 Mountain Spyder was a powerful dwarf. 3.45 metres long, weighing 384 kilograms, with a 275-hp engine. Here Rolf Stommelen is waiting to start on Mont Ventoux.

47__ Porsche 908/03

A Pure Driving Machine

Porsche celebrates big racing successes with a "victory poster". The poster after the 54th Targa Florio on 3 May 1970 gets the pulse racing. A light blue car is hurtling towards the camera with a cloud of grey dust behind it. Two orange arrows on the flat, broad body are pointing in the direction of motion. The driver's red helmet with a white cross tells insiders that Jo Siffert, one of the fastest and most fearless, is at the wheel. A wall of people lines the road – that was usual in those days.

At this Targa, Siffert and the British driver Brian Redman took turns at the wheel. Nothing could resist their Porsche 908/03. It had been made specially for orgies of bends like this race in Sicily or the north loop of the Nürburgring. Those were the only places where the works car competed in 1970 and 1971. A highly compact Spyder with a short wheelbase and short overhangs, looking almost as wide as it was long. The bodywork yielded to slight pressure with a finger: foam-reinforced plastic, weighing twelve kilograms. Everything about this car had to be lightweight. In front of the rear axle, the eight intake funnels of the 350 hp, air-cooled, three-litre boxer engine project from the body. The seat is practically over the front axle. Somewhere in the delicate-looking space frame are the pedals. The driver, engine and gears right up front – a fantastic way to distribute the car's weight of approximately 550 kilograms. And it required nerves of steel on the part of the driver.

After the victory in Sicily, the 908/03 also won at the Nürburgring. In 1971 Porsche took this compact powerhouse back to the Targa, but had to pull out after accidents. At the Nürburgring, by contrast, the 908/03 was invincible in that year. Right into the 1980s, customers used this car successfully, sometimes with considerably more powerful engines. And to this day, the engineers vie with the drivers in their enthusiasm for a pure driving machine.

___ The Targa Florio in Sicily in 1970: Brian Redman is on the way to victory in this legendary road race in a 908/03. The Porsche was specially built for orgies of bends.

___ The nose of a Porsche 908/03
after the 1,000-kilometre race
at the Nürburgring in 1970,
sand-blasted by stones thrown up
by the other cars.

48___ Porsche 917 PA Spyder 16-Cylinder

A Giant that Couldn't Walk

Porsche was unbeatable in 1972 and 1973 with the 917/10 and the 917/30 in the Canadian-American Challenge Cup – CanAm for short. But before these racing cars with their 12-cylinder turbo generators could set out on the road to victory, engine evolution had to make a dinosaur extinct.

The story began in 1969, when Jo Siffert, a driver in the Porsche works team, first tried the CanAm. His enthusiasm for the extremely popular 200-mile sprints beyond the Atlantic was infectious in Zuffenhausen. Two open 917s were made. With one of these 917 PA Spyders – PA stands for Porsche Audi Division, VW North America –Siffert competed in the USA. He gave a good account of himself, but it was clear that in a 775-kilogram Porsche even a driving genius like Siffert could not keep up with a 670-kilogram McLaren, Lola or Chaparral. Especially because he was under-powered with his 560 hp from a 4.5-litre 12-cylinder engine. The Americans were driving V8 Chevrolets with seven-litre engines producing well over 600 hp.

Zuffenhausen worked its magic, and in 1970–71, alongside the world championship programme and Le Mans, developed the biggest racing engine in Porsche history: air-cooled, 16 cylinders, two valves, 6.5-litres and 755 hp. Three of them were made. In August 1971 one of these giants was put into the back of a PA Spyder. The test drivers said it was good to handle and performed well. But this 16-cylinder engine weighed 320 kilograms and was 25 centimetres longer than a 12-cylinder version. The frame of the 917 PA Spyder had to be reinforced and the car's weight rose to 845 kilograms. And, as things happen in evolution, an alternative emerged for the same purpose: a 12-cylinder turbo engine, 4.5 litres, weighing only 270 kilograms and generating 850 hp. This sealed the fate of the 16-cylinder monster: a place in the museum.

___ This is the biggest racing engine ever developed by Porsche. The air-cooled 16-cylinder motor generated 755 hp with its 6.5-litre capacity – and was never used in a race.

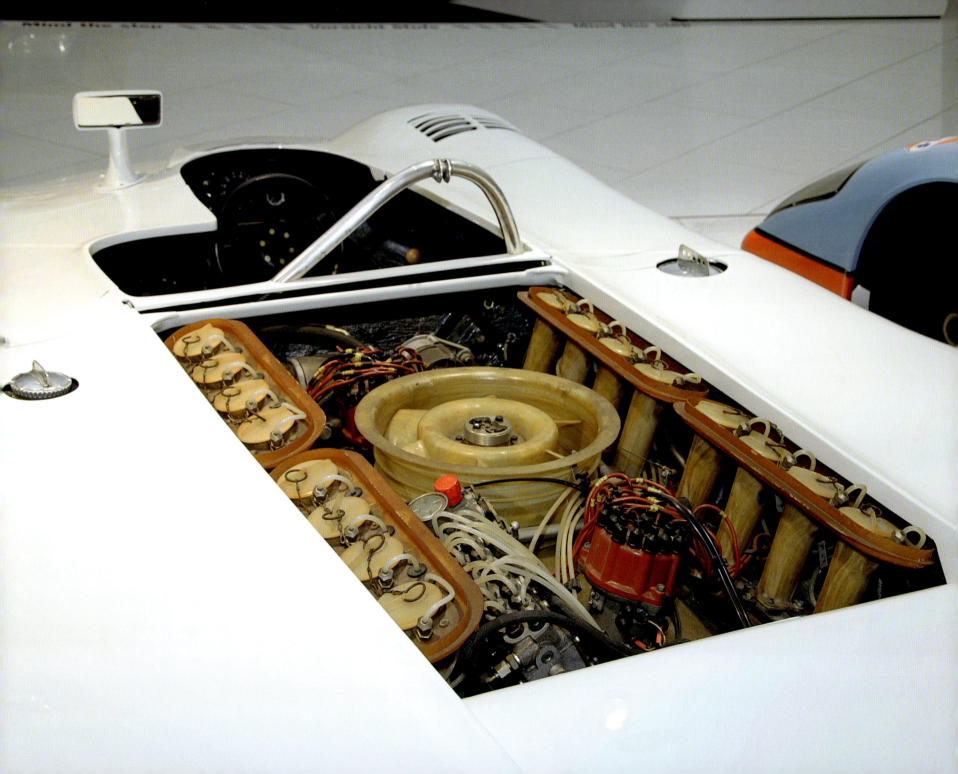

49__ Porsche 917/30 Spyder

The Monster

Even dyed-in-the-wool Porsche fans raised their eyebrows. "Acceleration 0 to 200 km/h in 5.4 seconds, 0 to 300 km/h in 11 seconds", said the description of the Porsche 917/30 Spyder in 1973. The Porsche motor-sports division had not bothered to name a figure for "0 to 100".

Everything about this racing car was extraordinary. Porsche had built it for the American-Canadian CanAm series, where complete technical freedom was allowed. "The sky is the limit" was the motto here, and Porsche took the organisers by their word. The 5.4-litre 12-cylinder engine of the 917/30 Spyder generated 1,200 hp with two turbos and catapulted 917/30 to a maximum speed of 385 km/h in spite of the huge rear spoiler on the plastic bodywork. Such a number of horses get amazingly thirsty. Thus the tank had to be generously sized at 400 litres, and Porsche calculated consumption at around 100 litres for 100 kilometres. With an empty tank, the 917/30 Spyder weighed 800 kilograms, which meant an insane weight-power ratio of almost 700 grams per horsepower. By way of comparison: on the first 911 Turbo for road traffic, which Porsche presented a year later, each horsepower moved 4.3 kilograms – and even this was regarded as awe-inspiring and hardly controllable by car testers at the time.

Against this massive power of the 917/30 Spyder, American competitors did not stand a chance. V8 normally aspirated engines with 8 litres and 750 hp suddenly seemed feeble. In six races the Porsche put in the fastest practice lap six times, scorched a new lap record into the asphalt every time, and won. This was too much for the racing establishment in the USA. For 1974 the CanAm came up with a limit on consumption for turbo engines, i.e. for Porsche, which suited the spirit of the times in the so-called "oil crisis". And after a short life, the monster became a fossil.

____ The Riverside race track in California in 1973. Two 917/30 Spyders in the pits. Despite the huge rear spoilers, the 1,200-hp Porsches reach a speed of 385 km/h.

50___ Porsche 935 2.0 "Baby"

The "Baby" with Winning Genes

The German racing championship in 1977: Porsche customers fight it out amongst themselves in the top class, as there is no competition. In the "small" division with engines of up to two litres, the Ford Escort and BMW 2002 are engaged in spectacular battles. Porsche is not involved here, and some said that they dare not. At this, Porsche boss Ernst Fuhrmann announced that the company would fly the flag in the small division at the most important race of the year at Nuremberg's Norisring. With a turbo, as that was Porsche's domain.

Only three months' time remained to get an engine working and slim down a 911 to the permitted 735 kilograms. There was a handicap for turbo engines: only 1.4 litres capacity were allowed in the two-litre class. Porsche's engine generated 370 hp at 8,000 rpm from 1,425 cubic centimetres. The car's weight-reduction programme was radical: instead of a floor of steel plate, the "935 2.0" had an aluminium frame. Light frames also held the tank and the axles. Plastic bodywork, titanium suspension and perforated pedals of light-metal reduced the weight further. The mechanics joked that the pointer of the revs counter should also have holes drilled in it. Finally the car was so light that the racing department filled low-lying supports with lead. It was easy to find a name for the lightest 911 with the smallest engine: "Baby".

On the Norisring Jacky Ickx was at the wheel. He was a tough man, not easily dismayed by anything. But it was scorchingly hot, and furthermore the engine and gearbox heated up the cockpit. This was too much even for Ickx. But at the second attempt, on the Hockenheimring, Porsche hit the straps. In practice Ickx lapped an unbelievable 2.8 seconds faster than the nearest competitor. "Baby" won the one-hour race with a lead of 58 seconds. Porsche had dared.

___ The Belgian driver Jacky Ickx drove "Baby" in pizza-oven temperatures on the Norisring at Nuremberg in 1977. The open window failed to help: Ickx and the 370-hp Porsche overheated.

51__ Porsche 935/78 "Moby Dick"

The Most Powerful 911 of All Time

The Porsche 911 is like a good Beatles song: there are infinite ways of interpreting it. The wildest version was created in 1978 for the World Sportscar Championship: the 935/78, which quickly acquired the nickname "Moby Dick" at Porsche. Like the great white whale, this car was terrifyingly strong and terrifyingly big (and rare, of course – there were only two of them). When the chips were down, its 3.2-litre twin charger – with a water-cooled four-valve head for the first time – turned out 845 hp (621 kW).

The streamlined body was 4.89 metres long, a good 60 centimetres longer than the metal exterior of a normal 911, and moreover "Moby Dick" was 30 centimetres wider. The 935/78 shrank only in terms of its height, by six centimetres, as the project manager Norbert Singer had (once again) come up with a clever interpretation of the technical regulations. The rules said that the flanks of the bodywork could be cut open – in order to make space for lateral exhaust pipes, for example. They did not specify how big the openings could be. So without further ado Singer's team hacked six centimetres from the bottom of the bodywork. The silhouette of the roof remained unchanged, as the rules required. This smaller head-on surface, coupled with aerodynamically superb bodywork, resulted in an astounding top speed of 366 kilometres per hour at Le Mans.

It hardly needs to be said that Moby Dick was a lightweight whale with plastic bodywork mounted on a fine tubular frame. On its first appearance, at Silverstone in England on 13 May, the 935/78 won the six-hour race with a lead of seven laps. In Le Mans an oil leak, faulty ignition and fuel consumption of over 90 litres per 100 kilometres pushed the car back to eighth place. There were only two more sightings of "Moby Dick" in its natural habitat, and then the monster was consigned to a place in the Porsche Museum.

____ "Moby Dick" was the most powerful and the fastest racing car based on the 911 that Porsche ever entered for a competition. 845 hp took it to over 360 km/h.

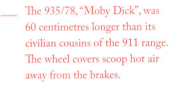

The 935/78, "Moby Dick", was 60 centimetres longer than its civilian cousins of the 911 range. The wheel covers scoop hot air away from the brakes.

52__ Porsche 956/962C

Serial Winner with the "Ground Effect"

27 March 1982, at the Porsche test circuit in Weissach. Jürgen Barth has completed his first laps with a new racing car and is delighted. No roll-out has ever gone so smoothly – after only nine months' development. The 956 is the first Porsche with an aluminium monocoque: instead of tubes, the chassis consists of riveted aluminium sheets, which is highly complicated but makes the construction incredibly stable.

And the way the 956 takes fast curves ... Barth has never seen anything like it in his racing life. The mechanics check the low-slung 630-hp machine: all okay. But what's this here? Dirt, grass, small stones on the underbody. "Jürgen, did you fly off the track somewhere?" No, he didn't, but the 956 has done exactly what project manager and aerodynamics guru Norbert Singer expected: from a speed of about 180 km/h the air pressure beneath the car became so low, thanks to the special underbody shape, that the downforce doubled the weight of the Porsche. 800 kilos of downforce were added to the vehicle's weight of 800 kilograms. This is called the "ground effect", and it was a revolution for sports cars. A few days later, the racing drivers Jacky Ickx and Jochen Mass had another very impressive experience on the Circuit Paul Ricard in the south of France: the huge downforce and blistering cornering speeds troubled even these two fearless men. It was some time before they kept their foot on the accelerator in curves.

The 956 was a leap forward, just like its successor, the 962C, which took part in the world championship from 1985 with a longer wheelbase and 700 hp from a three-litre engine. The results were overwhelming: six Le Mans wins between 1982 and 1987, five drivers' championships, six for the marque and one for the team. From 1987 Porsche turned to other fields of sporting activity. The revolutionary 956 became a much-loved museum exhibit.

____ Boy, oh boy! From speeds of around 180 km/h the 956 can drive under the ceiling, thanks to an enormous ground effect. In the Porsche Museum strong bolts do the job.

Spee

Was nützen Hunderte von PS, wenn sich die Leis-
tung nicht in Geschwindigkeit umsetzen lässt? Eine ausgefeilte
Aerodynamik ist einer der entscheidenden Faktoren für
die Schnelligkeit.

speed?
ano
the t

Denn wenn Motorleistung und Fahrzeuggewicht iden-
tisch sind, spielt im Vergleich zweier Fahrzeuge die Karosserie
eine wichtige Rolle. Je weniger Luftwiderstand sie bietet, um
so schneller kann man fahren. Porsche hat das immer wieder bei
Rennen wie den 24 Stunden von Le Mans bewiesen. Aerodynamische Hilfsmittel wie Unterboden und Flügel sorgen dafür, dass
Rennwagen hohe Geschwindigkeiten erreichen, aber trotzdem
noch für die Fahrer kontrollierbar bleiben.

equa
the L
As At
st
ano
f

Schon Ferdinand Porsche versucht, seine Fahrzeuge
schnell und zugleich beherrschbar zu machen. Das Zauberwort
heißt: aerodynamische Effizienz. Sie entsteht durch das
Verhältnis von erwünschter Bodenhaftung („Abtrieb") zu
unerwünschtem Luftwiderstand.

Bei einem Sportwagen auf der Straße ist das nicht
anders, so wird der 911 Carrera RS 2.7 zum schnellsten Serien-
sportwagen seiner Zeit. Die Faustformel von Porsche bleibt
unverändert: maximale Fahrleistungen durch optimale
Aerodynamik.

53__ TAG Turbo V6 made by Porsche

A Dwarf with the Strength of a Giant

The 5.4-litre twin turbo of the Porsche 917/30 in 1973 generated 1,200 hp and weighed 280 kilograms. In August 1983 a McLaren Formula 1 started the Netherlands Grand Prix with a Porsche engine that seemed a midget by comparison.

The TAG Turbo made by Porsche was a V6 with 1499 cc capacity and a weight of 150 kilograms. But this dwarf gave out 720 hp. By the end of the year that would increase to 1,040 horsepower. The power per litre of engine capacity amounted to about 222 hp on the 12-cylinder giant, and for the Formula 1 midget an incredible 693 horsepower. The Porsche engine expert Hans Mezger and his team had designed both engines and made clever use of advances in technology, materials and electronics for the TAG engine. By means of a cooling method specially invented for the V6, no fuel had to be sacrificed to keep the engine temperatures low, as competitors at Alfa Romeo, BMW, Renault and Ferrari did. Small losses from friction and precise electronic engine management contributed to the top performance, with low, easily calculated consumption. In contrast to its rivals, McLaren therefore set off without a safety reserve of petrol – a major advantage in Formula 1, where every single gram of weight counts.

The Porsche engine, financed by the businessman Mansour Ojjeh and his company Techniques d'Avant Garde (TAG), and the chassis of the McLaren MP4 proved to be a successful combination. In their first full year of racing, 1984, McLaren-Porsche won twelve Grands Prix out of 16 that they entered. The McLaren driver Niki Lauda won the drivers' championship ahead of his team-mate Alain Prost. In 1985 Prost took the title, and McLaren won the constructors' championship again. In 1986 the history of this little V6 extremist came to an end, after 25 Grand Prix victories, with a further champion's title for Prost.

___ It was compact, strong as a lion and not especially thirsty. The TAG Turbo V6 made by Porsche was a major coup in Formula 1 between 1984 and 1986.

54__ Porsche 919 Hybrid

Extremely Complex, Extremely Fascinating

The Porsche works driver Brendon Hartley called the 919 Hybrid the "most complex racing car in the world". The Le Mans prototype for the endurance world championship won the 24 Hours of Le Mans, the most important race in the series, in 2015, '16 and '17. The championship is about speed and the future of the automobile, which is why the rule-makers take a diabolical delight in reducing the permitted fuel consumption every year and making hybrid power compulsory. The principle that applies here is that the more electrical energy is produced per lap and converted into propulsion, the less petrol the internal combustion engine may consume.

Porsche entered the highest "megajoule efficiency class". This means lots of electric power and not much petrol. The company combined a V4 direct-injection two-litre engine, with a turbocharger and around 500 hp, with a 400 hp electric motor. The V4 drives the rear axle, the electric motor the front wheels. Porsche had a unique idea for generating electric power: under braking, kinetic energy is captured at the front axle and converted to electricity. In the exhaust tract, a turbine drives a generator that provides additional power for the lithium-ion battery. Electronics directs the complex interaction of the engines, brakes, chargers, battery and power distribution. The result was an 875-kilogram racing car with smart four-wheel drive and just under 1,000 hp. This may sound dry as dust, but it is a spectacular sight when the 919 Hybrid accelerates from the bend or brakes for a chicane from 340 km/h.

In its victory at Le Mans in 2015 the Porsche consumed a little over 34 litres of petrol per 100 kilometres at an average speed of 224.2 km/h. Pretty damn fine, said the rule makers, but not good enough. And for 2016 they allowed the engineers eight per cent less fuel. Porsche won again.

___ Away and out of sight: with this 919 Hybrid, Porsche won the hat trick at the 24 Hours of Le Mans from 2015 to 2017. Thanks to an electric motor and a combustion engine, it was powered by 1,000 hp.

___ 24 Hours of Le Mans, 2015:
what happened to those
beautiful old streamlined cars?
The wind tunnel requires
strange aesthetics.

——— Showtime in the Porsche Pits at Le Mans 1967. The young ladies are advertising a tyre company. But once the race is on, playtime is over. It's time for big decisions.

AT THE PITWALL

55__ Fritz Huschke von Hanstein

Man of the World and PR Genius

The 24 Hours of Le Mans race in 1953. The little 550 RS Spyder may not have a role in the struggle for first place, but reporters are coming and going at Porsche. Huschke von Hanstein, head of press relations and racing manager for a year now, has cleverly exploited a faux pas by the race organisers. There were too few workplaces for journalists. Hanstein installed them in the Porsche pits. A year later, a 550 Spyder sped to third place at the Carrera Panamericana in Mexico. Sponsors' logos adorned the aluminium bodywork – an innovation in motor racing, introduced by von Hanstein. The entry of a Porsche 911 in the Monte Carlo Rally in 1965 was primarily intended as a delivery to the prince, whom Hanstein wanted to acquire a taste for the car. The fact that the Italian Barone Pucci was sometimes allowed to do a race in a works Porsche had less to do with his talent as a driver than with something that von Hanstein knew: "As long as he drives for us, none of our cars will be stolen in Italy." And in the 1970s, when a scrutineer in Le Mans wanted to refuse starting permission to a Porsche, von Hanstein knew that it was the man's birthday. Congratulations, a short chat, perhaps a small present ... and the Porsche took part.

Huschke von Hanstein: a gentleman and man of the world, who won races and championships himself, and broke world records, played a decisive role in shaping the company's public image into the 1960s. A masterly diplomat and a passionate communicator, he was honoured by his drivers with the presentation of a golden telephone. In 1956 he officially registered his nickname "Huschke" as his first name: Fritz Sittig Enno Werner, Baron von Hanstein, as he was christened on 3 January 1911 in Halle an der Saale, seemed a bit unwieldy. The "racing baron" died on 5 March 1996 in Stuttgart.

____ Always perfectly styled, always a gentleman: from 1952 to 1968 Huschke von Hanstein, head of press relations and racing manager, had a vital part in shaping the Porsche company image.

56__ Wilhelm Hild

The Man with the broken Cigarette

He insisted on doing it himself. Even at the biggest and most important races, Wilhelm Hild personally filled the works cars with petrol. Usually wearing a long coat, a hat on his head and horn-rimmed glasses. Some say: and with a cigarette. But that is probably a legend. Yet the fact is that Hild was a passionate smoker who broke his cigarettes in two halves before lighting them – an economy measure. The company newspaper "Christophorus" commented on a photo from the 1950s with the following caption: "A rare shot, because engineer Hild appears on this photo without a cigarette …"

Born on 13 May 1909, Hild came to Porsche in 1943 from Auto Union, where he had designed and operated racing cars for DKW. In Zuffenhausen, under head of development Karl Rabe, Hild was first of all occupied with diesel engines and tractors. When the design office moved to Gmünd in 1944, Hild followed and worked on the Porsche diesel truck, but then kept faith with motor racing. He played a significant part in developing the compressor engine for the Cisitalia Grand Prix car.

When the company returned to Stuttgart, Wilhelm Hild's career as the leading racing engineer at Porsche began. The racing engineer was the person in the test department responsible for assembly, testing and operation of the racing cars – the technical head of racing, one could say. Hild was the man behind the first 356 SL and 550 coupés at Le Mans, and the Formula 2 and Formula 1 Type 804 in the early 1970s. He was in charge of the expeditions to Sebring, Daytona and the Targa Florio. Hild did these things his own way. His successor, Peter Falk, recalled that "Even on the longest journeys of our transporters to Sicily, there was always a 356 driving at the back of the convoy. Inside it was Hild, who kept his eye on everything in this way." Wilhelm Hild died on 27 August 1973.

___ Wilhelm Hild (right) and Hans Mezger at the Nürburgring in 1962. Hild was present at the start-up of Porsche and became the company's first chief racing engineer.

57___ Peter Falk

A Quietly Successful Head of Racing

Peter Falk's application for a job at Porsche was 15 lines long. Born in 1932, graduate in engineering from Stuttgart Technical University, bodywork specialist, motor sports experience. Falk was a man of few words. Porsche took him on.

From 1959 his home was the experimental department that, in the course of endless tests, turns the raw form of a sports car into a machine of delight. Falk was in the small team that put the 911 on the road. As the experimental testing department was also the Porsche racing department, Falk could keep faith with his second passion. From autumn 1964 he was head of pre- and racing development, and until the end of the sixties converted the ideas of head of technology Ferdinand Piëch into victories and championships. From 1970 Falk headed drive testing and had less time for racing, but was present at the tracks as the man behind the success. From 1981 he established the first department devoted purely to racing. Between 1982 and 1988, under Falk's leadership this department won four endurance world titles, five team and driver world championships and four 24 Hours of Le Mans with the 962C car. And the Paris–Dakar Rally, twice. The TAG engine took McLaren to three drivers' and two constructor's titles – to name only the greatest triumphs.

Never again did Porsche manage to run a racing programme like this. In the late 1980s business conditions deteriorated, and motor sports took second place. So Falk devoted himself to production cars again. The next 911 generation – the 993 – needed a new suspension, so things came full circle. As a boy he had added a proper suspension to his toy truck, and as an apprentice Falk rode his bicycle to Daimler with a full suspension designed by himself. In late 1992, at the age of 60, he said farewell – a promise to his wife Ruth, who once said "My husband is married to Porsche."

___ Le Mans 1983: Peter Falk (right) is issuing instructions. The listeners are (left to right) head of development Helmuth Bott, racing engineers Norbert Singer and Klaus Bischof.

58__ Hans Mezger

Who Made the Horses Gallop

TAG Turbo, made by Porsche and Hans Mezger. The Formula 1 engine that took the McLaren team to 25 Grand Prix victories, with which Niki Lauda in 1984 and Alain Prost in 1985 and 1986 shot to world championship titles. And the man who designed this technical masterpiece. Hans Mezger is a Porsche man through and through.

After graduating in mechanical engineering, he started at Zuffenhausen on 1 October 1956. He was 26 years old. For 37 years, his entire professional life, Mezger stayed with the company. Fans and experts know and admire him for his Formula 1 powerhouse, but before that Mezger had already established milestones in developing engines. With Ferdinand Piëch he was part of the small team that designed the six-cylinder boxer engine with dry-sump lubrication for the first 911 – an engine that, like the 911, harboured extraordinary potential for development and remained modern right into the 21st century. In 1968, when Ferdinand Piëch more or less single-handedly set in motion a project, the 917 racer, that was financially and technically extremely risky, but then also overwhelmingly successful in sporting terms, Mezger headed the design team and drew up plans with his staff for the harmless-sounding Type 912, the most powerful racing engine that Porsche had ever made. Porsche's hp figures were ramped up even further by the company's involvement in the American CanAm series from 1972. Here Hans Mezger as designer and Valentin Schäffer as developer redefined turbo technology and made Porsche a non-stop winner.

Success at motor sports opened the door for a further Porsche coup: the 911 Turbo, which made history as the first German super sports car. Turbo technology remained the key to success for Porsche, in motor sports as elsewhere – from Le Mans to the TAG. Hans Mezger went into retirement on 1 October 1993.

___ Hans Mezger (left), here seen in Weissach in 1983, was famous in the motor-sports world for designing the 12-cylinder engine for the Porsche 917 and the TAG Turbo Formula 1 engine.

59__Jürgen Barth

Diplomacy at Racing Speed

It had to happen! Jürgen Barth's father Edgar was one of the best German racing drivers, who won for Porsche the Targa Florio and also the European hillclimb championship three times: in 1959, 1963 and 1964. Jürgen was ten years old in 1957 when his father let him take the wheel of a 356 on the Nürburgring North Loop. It was only logical that Jürgen learned his trade from scratch at Porsche, beginning in 1963: mechanic, a commercial apprenticeship, then a technician's diploma. At 22 Barth was already assistant to Huschke von Hanstein, head of press relations and sports. Like his boss, Barth contested rallies and races. From von Hanstein he learned the fine art of motor-sports diplomacy: how to handle officialdom, team bosses and sponsors.

Soon he was representing Porsche all round the world, but again and again he got into the cockpit and drove everything, from the 911 to the 908/03 and 917. In 1977 Barth won Le Mans. With velvet gloves and nerves of steel he nursed a dying Porsche 936 to the chequered flag. From 1982 the all-rounder Barth was head of customer sports. Le Mans that year was a typical case. He organised the works team on the spot, and smoothed over a conflict with the main sponsor, because the team's outfit was delayed in customs. When the driver Hurley Haywood ran out of steam at two in the morning and fell back in the 956, Barth took the wheel, moved up the field and caught up with the two leading team-mates: a triple victory. In 1992 Barth was one of three men who initiated a GT race series, ushering in the renaissance of Grand Touring cars on racing tracks. In 1994 he was an organiser of the first international motor race in China.

Into the 21st century Barth shaped motor racing in committees and organisations. But what makes him look truly happy is to put on his driver's overalls and slip into the cockpit of a magnificent old racing car.

____ Jürgen Barth sprays the champagne in Le Mans in 1977. He won the race together with Hurley Haywood (right) and Jacky Ickx (second from left).

60__ Norbert Singer

Master of the Air

Norbert Singer, born in 1939, was always good for a surprise. He studied aerospace technology in Munich, then vehicle engineering, coming to Porsche in 1970 as a young graduate.

Singer became famous for his skill at interpreting technical regulations in such a way that those who wrote them were amazed and Porsche won races. And his genius in handling air currents took Porsche to several world championships. There was the 935 with the double rear window – one above the other, which made the back of the racing 911 highly streamlined. The rule book said that the rear could not be altered, but it didn't say that nothing could be fitted above it. The result: five World makes Championship titles. And then there was the 935/78, "Moby Dick", at the sight of which even Porsche employees wondered what this was. In 1982 Singer's team of engineers developed the next revolution: thanks to special aerodynamics, the Porsche 956 achieved cornering speeds that had previously been impossible. By 1986 the "ground effect" racing car had won ten world championships. In 1996 Singer was the project manager who sent the first mid-engine 911 onto the race track.

As a racing strategist, too, Norbert Singer made a name for himself on countless days and nights at tracks around the world. And as a mentor for young drivers who had infinite know-how and a great deal of patience. Yet sometimes even Singer ran out of patience. At Porsche they still tell the story of the racing driver who failed to achieve good times in the decisive qualifying laps. Singer altered everything on the car, then changed it back again. Finally the despairing driver asked: "What more should I do?" Singer gave him a long look and said: "Son, just put your foot down." In December 2004 Norbert Singer said his farewells, and is still regarded with affection and respect in the world of motor sports.

__ Norbert Singer (left) invented winners such as the 956 and 935 and was regarded as a cunning racing strategist. Here he is talking to Hans-Joachim Stuck (centre) and Rolf Huber.

A gem of a birthday gift. Ferry Porsche presented the first 911 Turbo to his sister Louise Piëch for her 70th birthday in 1974. The celebration was held in Dellach on the lake Wörthersee.

FAMILY JEWELS

61__ Porsche 356 1100 Coupé "Ferdinand"

Automobile Longevity

From March 1950 the first Porsche sports cars were made in Stuttgart-Zuffenhausen, following the company's return from Gmünd in Carnatia, where "Porsche Konstruktionen GmbH" had been moved in autumn 1944. By the end of the year "Dr. Ing. h.c. F. Porsche KG", as it was now called, had manufactured 369 units of the 356 with 108 employees.

One of these first 356s with sheet-steel bodywork – the few Porsches made in Gmünd had aluminium bodies – was the coupé with chassis number 5056. Ferdinand Porsche was given the car with a 1.1-litre boxer engine and 40 hp, the series standard, as a 75th birthday present on 3 September. The company patriarch died in January 1951. The coupé, which had a top speed of around 140 km/h, covered some 300,000 kilometres as a test car in the following eight years. At that time, all Porsche test cars had names. There was the "Greyhound", "Adrian" – and now "Ferdinand". Like the man it was named after, the car was extremely open to technical innovations. In "Ferdinand" Porsche tested, for example, a anti-roll bar and rack-and-pinion steering that was not to enter series production until 1965 in the 911. In 1955 "Ferdinand" travelled for test drives on radial tyres, which were then ground-breaking, and was the first Porsche 356 to be powered by a "Carrera engine", the four-camshaft power source that was designed for racing.

A reminder to this day of "Ferdinand's" eventful history and diverse variations as a mobile test lab is the steering-wheel hub with the Porsche coat of arms, installed after first production, which was not designed until 1952 and appeared in series-production sports cars from 1954 onwards. Connoisseurs delight in the balsa-wood gear knob, which Porsche quoted as a style feature in the Carrera GT super sports car presented in 2002. Today "Ferdinand" is in the Porsche Museum in Stuttgart.

__ Ferdinand with Ferdinand: the eponymous company founder (left) had driven his birthday present over the dusty roads of the Katschbergpass in Austria in 1950.

62__ Porsche 911 Turbo No. 1

Tartan and 260 hp

This unique piece of family treasure was given by Ferry Porsche to his sister Louise Piëch on the occasion of her 70th birthday. A plaque on the glove compartment is engraved with the following words: "LP Turbo-Porsche No. 1 Stuttgart-Zuffenhausen 29 August 1974."

The first 911 Turbo approved for road traffic was an object lesson in understatement. The silver bodywork corresponded to that of the 911 Carrera and thus had no need of the widened wings of the later 911 Turbo. The bonnet bears the "Carrera" lettering instead of "Turbo". Only the big tail spoiler corresponded to that of the muscular sports car that Porsche was then to present in its definitive version at the Paris Auto-Salon in October 1974. In terms of its engine, Louise Piëch's Turbo differed a good deal from the latter, as this jewel was handed over to her with a 240 hp (176 kW), 2.7-litre naturally aspirated engine – an improved-performance variation on the engine from the famous 911 Carrera RS 2.7. This engine was, however, soon to be replaced by a three-litre turbo that delivered 260 hp (196 kW). The Porsche lettering on the sides has a tartan background that is repeated in the interior. The cosy red produces an interesting contrast to the revs counter, whose scale goes up to a frightening 10,000 rpm and is reminiscent of the 911 Carrera RSR Turbo 2.1 that had been causing a sensation in the World Sportscar Championship since April of that year and took second place at Le Mans in June 1974.

Louise Piëch was not only an extremely successful businesswoman, but also an art historian and painter. She loved to tour the most beautiful areas of her Austrian homeland in her sports car, and to take up the artist's brush while still in the cockpit. That is the reason why the "Turbo-Porsche No. 1", in contrast to future series-built versions, has no tinted-glass windows.

___ A muscular sports car with floral decoration. In 1974 Ferry Porsche presented the first 911 Turbo to his sister Louise Piëch as a birthday gift. Here the official presentation is being prepared.

63__914/8

Dr Jekyll for Doctors Porsche & Piëch

With this Dr Jekyll it was hardly possible to see the Mr Hyde. Unless you had a closer acquaintance with the Porsche 914. Yes, the wheel housings had been enlarged somewhat. And that oval opening at the nose, with an oil cooler behind it. Those who took a closer look became pensive: the roof did not consist of the usual plastic but of metal. And it had been welded to the windshield frame and the roll-over bar. All of this had been done discreetly, but one thing was clear: this was no standard VW Porsche with a four- or six-cylinder engine.

Then the gentleman with the slightly wavy grey hair gets into the mid-engine sports car. Isn't that? Yes, it is: Dr Ferry Porsche. The door closes, he turns the ignition key. Wow! That definitely sounds like motor sports. Which is what it was: the employees had presented their boss with a special 914 for his 60th birthday in 1969. In front of the rear axle of the 914/8 S-II growled a not-quite-tamed, three-litre, eight-cylinder racing engine that could produce 260 hp at 7,700 revs. Things were even wilder under the bonnet of test boss Ferdinand Piëch's 914/8 S-I. Behind the seats was an even hotter version of the racing engine, with 300 hp that operated at 8,200 revolutions. After six seconds Piëch's unique "people's Porsche" rocketed from zero to 100 km/h, maxing out at over 250 km/h. Mr Hyde revealed himself above all acoustically and with powerful centrifugal forces, before disappearing from view at an impressive velocity.

In the early seventies Porsche assessed the opportunity for actually going into series production with an Über-914. The idea was that the 916 would have a top speed of 230 km/h with the 190-hp boxer of the 911 S. In fact the car would have been much too expensive. In the end only eleven prototypes were made, five of which found a home in the family treasure-vaults of the Porsches and Piëchs.

___ This is understatement: this Porsche 914 has hidden depths – for example, a racing engine with 260 hp. Ferry Porsche (second from left) is pleased with the little gem.

64_ Porsche Panamericana

An Exotic Automobile for the Future

Porsche Panamericana? A concept car dating from 1989, of which two were built. One was presented to Ferry Porsche on his 80th birthday, while the other was shown at the motor show in Frankfurt, where it provoked vehement debate. Critics saw it as an agglomeration of design quotes "without the appearance of maturity and coherence, and without balanced proportions", as a trade journal noted.

The intake vents in the nose had been known to the critics since the 911R in the late 1960s, and the slits in the bonnet derived from the first 901! The double domed roof was familiar from racing 911s, the detachable rear window from the 911 RS of the Safari Rally in the seventies. What was the point of the leather cover with a zip on the roof? And those free-standing buggy wheels! The Panamericana was indeed a provocation, because it looked completely different. And indeed the Panamericana was forward-looking. The bodywork was partly made of carbon-fibre-reinforced plastic. The detachable roof was present in very similar form, though with a glass cover that could slide to the back, in the 911 Targa of 1995–96. In front of the rear axle, the bodywork curved to a "waist" – a design feature of the next 911 generation, just like the flat front wings.

Were the small, speedster-like windshield, the free-standing wheels and the enormous ride-height a greeting to the fans of high-end buggies in California? It was reported that head designer Harm Lagaaij, who had come to Porsche in 1989, had wanted a mini-series, and the West Coast of the USA would have been the ideal playground for this car with 250 hp and the four-wheel drive of the Carrera 4. In the late 1980s, however, a sales crisis set in owing to the ailing US dollar. For Porsche this was to be a fight for survival. The company lacked the resources to make dreams come true, and the Panamericana ended up as a rare and exotic study.

___ The Panamericana looked exotic in 1989 and was full of good ideas for the future. This study in fresh-air driving belonged to Ferry Porsche's family jewels.

MAGIC WORDS

Speedster: from 1954 this word enchanted fans of motor racing in the USA. Competitors from England looked dowdy against this light, minimal Porsche.

65__ Gmünd

Cradle and Refuge

Gmünd in Carnatia, Austria: close to the Hohe Tauern and Nockberg mountains, outstanding terrain for testing sports cars. But first of all it was a refuge for the Porsche design office in November 1944, fleeing Allied bombing raids on Stuttgart. The armaments authorities had ordered the company, important to the war effort, to move. In Gmünd Porsche occupied the site of a timber yard, "W. Meineke Holzgrossindustrie Berlin-Gmünd", a large number of small buildings and halls. The staff of 300 called their new place of work the "United Hut Factory".

During the war, Porsche continued work on the Volkswagen, on tractors and military commissions like a all-terrain "Kübelwagen", a gas turbine and components for the V2 "flying bomb". The office designed sports-car versions of the Beetle on its own account, and shortly after the end of the war, the future direction that the company would take emerged: in 1946 the bodywork specialist Erwin Komenda made draughts of the Type 352, which already had the looks of the later 356 sports car. Ferry Porsche continued his father's tradition of sports and racing cars, and in 1947 designed the Type 360 Grand Prix racing car for the Italian industrialist Piero Dusio. In the summer of that year the Type 356 "VW Sports Car" took shape on the drawing board. And in summer 1948 the 356 Number 1 was ready to drive, though this mid-engine roadster was to be a one-off. Manufacture of the first small series of 52 rear-wheel-drive Porsche 356s with hand-made aluminium bodywork – partly using components from stranded "Kübelwagen" – started up a little later. Thus the first step from being a design office to a sports car marque was taken.

In 1950 Porsche returned to Stuttgart, and in March 1951 the gates of the site in Gmünd were closed. Today a private museum in Gmünd is a reminder of the Porsche years there.

___ In Gmünd Porsche made the first sports cars in the 356 series. In the background is the 356-001, in the foreground a 356/2 coupé: two classics on one photo.

66__ Carrera

An Honorary Title for Very Special Porsche Cars

The Spanish word "Carrera" has many meanings: from "beam" and "ladder" (in tights) to "course of study" and professional ladies of the night. "Piston stroke" gets us very close to our subject. For us, "Carrera" stands for car races and extremely special Porsches.

This is how it happened: the Carrera Panamericana was held in 1954 for the fifth and last time. This crazy road race, the sixth in the World Sportscar Championship, ran 3,070 kilometres from Tuxtla Gutiérrez in south-east Mexico to Ciudad Juárez on the US border. The Italian driver Umberto Maglioli won in a works Ferrari with a five-litre engine and 330 hp at an average speed of 173.7 km/h, ahead of another giant-engine vehicle from Maranello. And then came a surprise: Hans Herrmann took third place in a Porsche 550/1500 RS Spyder! A newly developed racing engine with 1.5 litres capacity and 110 hp catapulted strong Hans and his 550-kilogram mini-car to a top speed of 220 km/h. With this agile mid-engine racer Herrmann managed an incredible average of 157 km/h. He had to, because the Guatemalan driver Jaroslav Juhan in the second works Porsche was hard on his heels, and finished the five days in fourth position, only 36 seconds behind him and ahead of two more Ferraris. Back in Stuttgart the mood was jubilant.

For those with the skills and knowledge, in 1955 Porsche fitted a Type 356 A road sports car with the engine of the winner from Mexico, designed by Dr Ernst Fuhrmann, and called this powerhouse the 356A 1500 GS Carrera. Up to the 906 Carrera 6 of 1966, the tradition of giving the name "Carrera" to all Porsches with this high-revving racing engine lived on. When the original Carrera engine was replaced in the late 1960s, Porsche ennobled very special sports cars with the "Carrera" title. The first of these was the 911 Carrera RS 2.7 in 1972.

____ Racing driver Hans Herrmann has every reason to laugh: with the Carrera engine in front of the rear axle, his 550 Spyder became a giant-killer.

67__Porsche Speedster

A Yoga Course Is Helpful

Speed + Roadster = Speedster: a word with a magical effect on Porsche fans, as "Speedster" focuses like a magnifying glass on the pure Porsche philosophy of fast driving. A Porsche Speedster was light with no frills, had fantastic brakes and a proper kick – but no heating or glove compartment, no comfortably upholstered seats or wind-down windows. The side windows were fitted into the body, the small windshield was screwed on. The tiny cloth roof kept out gusts of wind but not the rain.

The idea for the Speedster came from Max Hoffman, the US importer, who needed a cheap, entry-level Porsche. As "Maxie" sold a third of Porsche production in 1954, he got what he wanted. The first Speedsters cost 2,995 dollars and were thus a shade cheaper than the British competitors Austin Healey, Jaguar and MG.

The 356 Speedster in 1954 got things started. Among Stuttgart officialdom, jaws dropped when Porsche presented its low-slung car for approval of the model: when the roof was closed, it was not possible to get in without pain or to remain seated without yoga training. But the car-mad youth of California were delighted. On weekdays they took the Speedster to university, at the weekend to the race track, where the Porsche was soon invincible. The Swabian-American idea of making a Porsche reduced to the minimum soon proved to be a stroke of genius, as the fans' adoration made the Speedster a legend.

55 hp, and later 70 or 75 hp, sufficed to bring out goose pimples below a flowing skirt in the 356 A Speedster. For the hard-bitten, Porsche had the Carrera Speedster with a racing engine and as much as 110 hp up its sleeve. It managed a reckless top speed of 200 km/h. In 1959 the original Speedster was taken out of the range, and it was not until 1987 that a 911 Speedster appeared at the IAA motor show. With a ridiculous top, hard as rock, and simply wonderful.

____ Until 1956 the AW registration plate stood for "Amerikanische Zone Württemberg", the German federal state where the Speedster was as rare as in the rest of Germany. No wonder, at a price of 12,000 deutschmarks.

68__ Downhill Racing

Torturing the Brakes on Mont Ventoux

"Downhill racing" – a word that prompts thoughts of dare-devil virtuosi of the ski slopes, the Streif in Kitzbühel, the Lauberhorn, the Tofana downhill straight at Cortina d'Ampezzo. Mont Ventoux is the mountain of pain in the Tour de France: 21 steep uphill kilometres, 1,612 metres of altitude in the hot winds of Provence.

Porsche test drivers combined "downhill racing" with Mont Ventoux. And the pain was felt by the Porsche brakes. Herbert Linge invented the first version of downhill racing when developing disk brakes in the 1960s. Initially on the Stilfser Joch in South Tyrol. Soon, however, too many tourist cars were on the roads in these mountains. An alternative was needed, as steep and full of bends as possible. It was found in the south of France, in Provence: voilà, Mont Ventoux. As long as anyone could remember, a run in the European Hillclimb Championship had been held there. In sports cars, racing cars and later in far-out prototypes, drivers stormed from the little town of Bédoin, south-west of the 1,912-metre mountain, up to the treeless summit with its meteorological station.

As the racing department at Porsche was simultaneously the testing department, a brakes specialist hit upon the idea of simply trying out this 21-kilometre run downhill. With no holds barred. This was one of the early secrets of the generally admired robustness of Porsche brakes. Even worse than the downhill race was the tourist downhill run, in high gear down Mont Ventoux with a fully laden Porsche. This not only hurt the brakes, but is said to have pained every test driver to the very core. What a good thing that Bédoin is situated among vineyards: consolation was never far away. In the late 1980s the test drives on Mont Ventoux came to an end, and Porsche now tests its brakes on the high-speed oval of Nardo in Italy, or on the testbed.

____ It's all downhill from here: a 911R on Mont Ventoux in the south of France in the late 1960s. The descent on this super twisty route was used as a lethal test of the brakes.

69__ Teloché

The Team HQ at the "Sharp Corner"

When getting the racing cars ready took a long time, late at night the Porsches thundered out of the little town of Teloché for a quick check on the country road, and came back ten minutes later along Rue du 8 Mai with a growling engine. In front of the little Garage du Provost the drivers switched off the engine, and the mechanics pushed the car into the workshop. This ritual took place for 30 years in Teloché, 2.8 kilometres as the crow flies from the Mulsanne Bend at the end of the long straight in Le Mans.

From the first race in 1951 until 1981, Teloché in the Département Sarthe was the navel of the Porsche motor sports universe for a week. In the Garage du Provost the 356 SL light-metal coupé, the powerful 917, the 935 and the 936/81 were all made ready. The workshop was a crowded place, and the long-tailed car bodies were stacked up in the backyard. The team slept in little pensions and rented private rooms, where ten shared a toilet and shower. The room furnishings were a bed and a chair, with a suitcase on the floor. Meals were taken in the Café du Sport at every time of day and night. Eating together was a sacred rite for the team, and everyone sat together, including the bosses. For a late-night drink they went one block further to the "Sharp Corner", as the Porsche people called the bar. The landlord and landlady lacked the stamina of Porsche mechanics and went to bed early, but the engine specialist Valentin Schäffer was the man entrusted with the key, and kept the bar open.

After the race, the team held celebrations in Teloché, or hung their heads as everything was packed up. From 1982 the racing cars became too specialised for the trip along the country road for the start, and therefore had to be made ready in the pits at the course. But Porsche veterans, on visits to Le Mans, still look in at Rue du 8 Mai.

___ Preparations for the 24 Hours of Le Mans in 1964. Although the workshop in the village of Teloché was cramped, the Porsche team came here every year from 1951 to 1981.

70__ Turbo

Horsepower from the Flow of Exhaust Gas

This is a magic word for technology fans. People who say "turbo" mean Porsche. This has become common since the 1970s, as Porsche reinvented the turbocharger for driving on routes with lots of bends. Turbo – to put it correctly, an exhaust turbocharger. A turbine rotates in the exhaust stream from an engine and drives via a shaft a compressor wheel that pushes air into the combustion chambers of the engine. A lot of air means a lot of oxygen, which means high performance and – voilà – a lot of horsepower from a small-capacity engine.

For ships, locomotives and racing engines in Indianapolis-style ovals, this worked well decades before Porsche came along. The captain, the train driver and the Indy driver, in contrast to a racing driver on the Nürburgring, used the brakes very sparingly. During braking the revs of the turbocharger plummet, the pressure and performance collapse, and it takes a little while when accelerating for them to come back up. This is where Porsche took action. Through clever regulation of the charging pressure, Porsche succeeded in making the turbocharger ever smaller and thus boosting the revs. The "turbo lag", the time between putting a foot on the gas and the kick from behind, became shorter.

Wherever a turbo Porsche competed in a race, it rained trophies – in 1972 and 1973 in the American CanAm series, from 1984 to 1986 in Formula 1. Of 18 overall wins at Le Mans up to 2016, 16 were achieved with turbo power. From 1975 the mighty 911 Turbo came to the fans, taking racing technology on to the roads. Porsche indefatigably refined the turbo technology: twin turbo, variable turbine geometry, electronics. Nowadays "turbo" is less about maximum power and more about downsizing, the trend to smaller engines with lower consumption generating horsepower that Porsche fans can get excited about.

____ The engine of a 911 Turbo on the test bed. From the early 1970s, Porsche made decisive advances in turbo technology for automobiles.

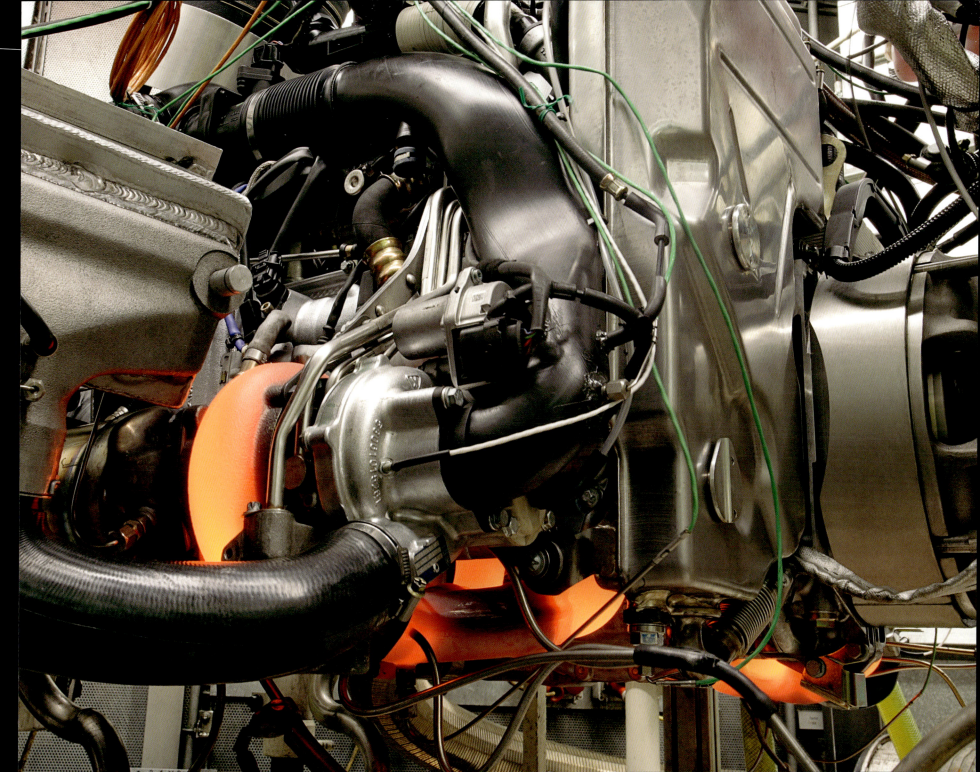

71__ Weissach

A High-Tech Centre on a Sheep Pasture

In 1959 Herbert Linge showed his boss Ferry Porsche 38 hectares of heathland, 25 kilometres north-west of Zuffenhausen. It lay between the villages of Weissach and Flacht, and yielded only thistles and sloes. Porsche was looking for space for test driving and an additional base for his company. He bought the land.

In 1961 construction of the first circuit began. When it was finished a year later, the local farmer and shepherd Robert Schüle took care of weeding and setting up pylons. He was Porsche's first permanent employee in Weissach. This idyllic start was followed by rapid growth of the Weissach Development Centre. The test track, wind tunnels, labs, workshops and studios cover 70 hectares today. Here the ideas of almost 6,000 engineers, technicians and other staff are crystallised into high-tech solutions and superb sports cars. In the best tradition of the first design office at Kronenstrasse 24 in Stuttgart, Porsche engineers in Weissach conceive and design technical solutions for a global clientele, from an Airbus cockpit to complete automobiles for other brands, and motors for Harley Davidson, fork-lift trucks or hospital beds. This work for other companies, most of it strictly confidential, is so successful that since 1996 Porsche Engineering has employed 1,000 engineers in Weissach alone to look after the needs of customers around the world.

Traditionally motor sports is also based in Weissach, which is therefore mentioned in the same breath as Le Mans or, recently, the "919 Hybrid". For the people of Weissach the nearby test track means they are sometimes ear-witnesses to the rollouts of new sports and racing cars. In addition to acoustic effects, there were financial benefits for the town right until 2015. Thanks to income from corporation tax paid by Porsche Weissach was Germany's richest community. Unfortunately these days have gone, as Porsche now belongs to the Volkswagen Group and the income stream was diverted to Wolfsburg.

____ The development centre in Weissach with an aerial view of the test track. In the foreground is the racing department near the village of Flacht, behind it the development centre.

Psychedelic art on a Porsche.
In 1970 head designer
Anatole Lapine created the
painted decoration of the
"hippie car". It was inspired
by his secretary's dress.

PORSCHE ART

72__Janis Joplin's 356 SC Cabriolet

Painted, Stolen, Salvaged

Janis Joplin was a superstar of the flower-power generation, a petite woman with a huge voice and a Porsche that looked as far-out as the clothes she wore. In September 1968 she bought a 1964 356 SC Cabriolet for 3,500 dollars. A fantastic sports car, except for the boring colour: pearl white. This was remedied by Dave Richards, a roadie who was handy with a brush and had already transformed her boyfriend's motorbike into a travelling psychedelic work of art. Joplin gave him 500 dollars for paint and artistic carte blanche. Richards adorned the Porsche with Janis' astrological sign, Capricorn, adding a rainbow, butterflies, jellyfish, the "eye of God" – he created "The History of the Universe".

Janis drove the 356 cabriolet for a year before it was stolen in San Francisco. The thief sprayed it grey. Nevertheless the cops quickly recovered Joplin's Porsche. The "History" was liberated from its sad grey covering and restored to its old, colourful glory. In autumn 1970 Janis recorded the album "Pearl" with her Full Tilt Boogie Band in Los Angeles. Then disaster struck. On 4 October she was found dead in her hotel room: heroin.

The Porsche was standing outside. Her manager drove the 356 until Janis's brother Michael and sister Laura claimed it for the family in 1973. Michael painted the car: grey! Sometimes Michael drove it, sometimes Laura, until the milometer stood at 140,000 and the car went into retirement. Then, in the early 90s, the Denver Center Theater Company discovered the Porsche as a requisite and restored the "History" painting in perfect, loving detail. Michael and Laura decided it was too good to drive and handed it over to the Rock and Roll Hall of Fame in Cleveland, Ohio in 1995. In 2015 Sotheby's auctioned Janis's Porsche. The auctioneer expected 600,000 dollars at most. On 10 December he banged his gavel at 1.76 million. Oh Janis, if only you could have cashed in.

___ Janis Joplins 356 SC Cabriolet "History of the Universe": hand-painted, unique, simply wonderful.

73__ Steve McQueen's "Le Mans"

From a Flop to a Legend

Steve McQueen had a vision: he wanted a documentary film about his passion: motor racing. In 1969 he turned up at the 24-hour race in Le Mans with 20 cameras. He showed his material to producers in the USA, but they turned him down. So McQueen founded Solar Productions. In 1970 he was back in Le Mans, bringing along a film crew and setting up his Solar Village close the race track. The artistic crowd enjoyed life there for a few months. To this day, in the Département Sarthe they tell stories about glittering parties and how the Yankees paid cash for everything, in dollars.

McQueen's family, too, was in France, but his children Chad and Terry were given private lessons in Château de Lornay, far away from the Dionysian solar colony. For the race McQueen entered his Porsche 908, in which he had competed in spring at Sebring with a broken leg from a motorbike incident and had finished second. The racing drivers Herbert Linge and Jonathan Williams drove the 908, with two cameras on board. This yielded ten kilometres of film with sensational action – all genuine, as computer-generated images didn't yet exist. After the race, the filming (and the parties in the Solar Village) continued until November. 40 drivers took the cockpit for McQueen, including big names such as Derek Bell, Vic Elford, Gérard Larrousse, Herbert Linge and David Piper. Several cars were shredded on the crash barriers.

In autumn the film was finished: the story of the racing driver Michael Delaney in a beautiful Porsche 917, Gulf design in pale blue and orange, and his German rival Erich Stahler, who lost the duel in a Ferrari 512S, which is why Ferrari made no cars available for filming. And McQueen was a few million dollars poorer. The world premiere of the movie was on 9 October 1971 – and it flopped. Today "Le Mans" is a cult film, just like the blue-and-orange 917. Art with a Porsche.

____ A break in shooting Steve McQueen's racing epic "Le Mans" in 1970. McQueen is sitting in a Porsche 917. The film flopped initially, but is now a cult movie.

74__ The 917 Hippie Car

Psychedelic Art at a Speed of 400

For the Le Mans race in 1970, Porsche's list of requests included a top speed of 400 km/h. Studies in the wind tunnel suggested bodywork with curves and round forms, which the designer Anatole Lapine thought extremely inspiring. In 1969 Lapine had taken the helm at Porsche Style. He designed a psychedelic paint job that seemed every bit as unreal as the idea of rocketing along between flimsy guide rails at 111 metres per second in a 550-hp beast. Lapine nonchalantly overlooked a rule of motor racing stipulating that the appearance of the car is determined by the sponsor's colours. The sponsor was Martini & Rossi, their colours yellow and red. But Lapine was set on purple and a poisonous-looking green. Fortunately Conte Rossi, a cultured man with an eye for art, gave his blessing.

As everything in motor sports happens at the last minute, the 917 arrived in Le Mans pure white, but Lapine was not discouraged. He and his artists went to work in the workshop backyard in the village of Teloché. First the purple. So in practice on the Thursday, Willi Kauhsen and Gérard Larrousse drove a purple-coloured 917 with white ornamentation round the course. By the Saturday, and several hundred spray cans later, a contemporary work of art had emerged, and the hippie Porsche rolled up to the starting line. The men from Porsche Style stood by the track, happy and tired, with aching index fingers. A red-and-white 917 gained the first Le Mans victory for Porsche, ahead of the second-placed hippie car.

The rest of story lacks glamour. The hippie 917 ended up in the wind tunnel, and the spontaneous art gave way to unpainted parts. A year later, completely repainted, the hippie chassis 043 competed at Le Mans again and was scrapped on 10 December 1971 at Porsche. All that remained were a few bodywork parts that Willi Kauhsen salvaged for his holiday home in Spain. And a pile of colourful photos.

____ 1970 was the era of flower power! And in Le Mans, Porsche art was on the move, sometimes at almost 400 km/h.

The spectators had eyes for nothing else when this psychedelic artwork raced past them at the 24 Hours of Le Mans in 1970.

75_ 917/20, the Sow

Big Bertha or Pig Bertha?

On 17 April 1971 the Porsche mechanics pushed a highly unusual racing car out of the pits for the pre-practice session for the 24 Hours of Le Mans. The 917/20 had neither the wedge-shaped short tail of the previous year's winner nor the almost endless bodywork of the long-tailed Porsche 917, designed for streamlining and high speeds. The 917/20 was full-bodied and curvaceous like a goddess painted by Rubens, and at 2.21 metres was 24 centimetres wider but 20 centimetres shorter than the short-tailed version. It did not fit inside any racing transporter and had to be taken to Le Mans on a flat-bed trailer for armoured vehicles.

In collaboration with the French aerodynamics specialist SERA, Porsche tried to put on the track a 917 that combined the advantages of the two bodywork versions: good road-holding and a brilliant top speed. The short-tailed car was relatively good at the first of these but maxed out at only 360, which was modest for Le Mans. The long version reached a wicked 386, but went as straight as a nervous viper. A name was soon found for this unique item: in blissful ignorance of recent history, the 600-hp racer was christened "Big Bertha".

For the race on 12 and 13 June a new name was called for, because Anatole Lapine's Porsche stylists had painted the car piglet-pink and labelled it in the style of a butcher: snout, neck, brain, cutlets and hams. "Zuffenhausen truffle hunter", said a little sticker. "The sow", which sounded more down-to-earth, was chosen. Willi Kauhsen and Reinhold Jöst put the sow round the course at a gallop, at times in third position. When Jöst lost control while breaking at the Arnage bend at 3:19 am on Sunday, they were lying sixth. So the sow won no prizes, but it was the most photographed car at this 24-hour event.

___ The "sow" in 1971 in the pits at Le Mans. "Let's go the whole hog", said the designers, and put butchers' labels on the pink beast.

76__ Porsche 911 Biggibilla

Songlines for a Carrera

This is a small excerpt from a huge culture, depicted on a Porsche. In 1998 the artist Biggibilla painted a 911 Carrera with motifs from the songlines passed on to him by his mother's brother. They are the songlines of the Gummaroi language group, which inhabits an area of 85,000 square kilometres in south-eastern Australia.

The songlines are chronicles of the origins, the walking trails, the life and death, the astronomy, the flora and fauna of an area, as each tribe of Aborigines handed them down over thousands of generations. The Gummaroi had more than 200 of these songlines, which helped them to gain orientation and to move around in the geo-graphy, the history and the mythology of their homeland: without maps, without a single written word. Biggibilla explains it as follows: "Those who do not know the songlines will never know the land. Our children learned their first songline at the age of five to eight years. It described some 200 different grasses, around 1,200 kinds of eucalyptus and 70 different moths and butterflies. The children learned approximately 7,000 words – for the first songline alone. By the time they grew up, they had learned about 140,000 words in the language of the men, 180,000 in the language of the women. Women spoke both languages, while men mastered only the male version."

There it stands, the 911 Carrera Biggibilla, presented to the headquarters in Stuttgart by Porsche Australia on the occasion of its 50th anniversary. With a wink of the eye, Biggibilla lent a further riddle to his mysterious painting: only the artist and Wendelin Wiedeking, Porsche CEO at that time, know where on the Porsche the artist's signature is to be found. The Porsche 911 Carrera Biggibilla is an exceptional work of art and an invitation to learn more about the fascinating culture of the Aborigines.

____ Melbourne in 1998: the artist Biggibilla explains to Porsche boss Wendelin Wiedeking motifs from the songlines of the Gummaroi language group.

77 _ Eleven Eleven

The Concrete Porsche

Classics attract interpretations. William Shakespeare has been worked over for centuries, Johann Sebastian Bach would be astonished to hear how his music is sometimes approached, and Ferdinand Alexander Porsche might possibly ask politely what it means when someone casts the silhouette of his 911 in concrete.

The Austrian artist Gottfried Bechtold loves to work in poured concrete. In 1971 he presented his own 911: an "everyday myth", as his called it at the time, cast in concrete. It was followed in 2001 by the "crash Porsche", also in concrete. In 2006 people on the square in front of the art gallery in Bechtold's home town of Bregenz were confronted with a sculptural group called "Eleven Eleven". Yes, you guessed it: eleven 911s in solid concrete. One of them weighed 16 tonnes, as much as eleven 911s. Bechtold explained to the Porsche magazine "Christophorus" that he was fascinated by the continued success and long-lived design of this iconic sports car. Both of these contradicted the fashion of rapid change. "Contradiction" – this seemed to be Bechtold's motto: "a car that can travel at 300 km/h, immobilised by the mass of the material", as "Christophorus" observed. The model for casting, too, was brought to a stop by Bechtold: he sent the 911 Carrera S to the metal press. All that remained was a cube of metal.

Alongside the unmistakeable silhouette and the high quality of craftsmanship, the genuine 911 and the eleven concrete ones have something else in common: "We went to the very limits of what is technically possible", Bechtold reported. The work took two years. Bechtold and his 25-strong team developed a special concrete mixture and processes for the work of art. Like all interpretations of classics, "Eleven Eleven" is an invitation to enjoy an argument about aesthetics, about sense and nonsense. It is certainly worth taking a look.

_____ An artistic interpretation of a classic automobile: Gottfried Bechtold cast the shape of a Porsche 911 in concrete. The work took two years to make.

The Batmobile? A UFO?
A villain's car? Nothing
of the kind: this car is a
racer and record-breaker.
From 1939 Porsche built
three Type 64 cars.

BIRDS OF PARADISE

78__ The Type 64

Founding Ancestor of the Porsche

Ferdinand Porsche had racing in his blood, and his designs for Mercedes-Benz and the Auto Union made motor-sports history. So it is not surprising that, at a time when the first prototypes of the Beetle were still undergoing endurance tests, sketches of hot Volkswagens with streamlined bodywork and engines with enhanced power were produced from the mid-1930s in his design office in Stuttgart.

Porsche turned to these drafts when Volkswagen commissioned him to design a racing car for the 1,680-kilometre competition from Berlin to Rome in September 1939. Porsche went all-out: the streamlined aluminium body designed by bodywork boss Erwin Komenda weighed in at 100 kilograms, only half that of standard sheet-steel skins, the side windows were of plastic, the steering column and pedals of aluminium. In order to limit the frontal area, the Type 64 was very narrow. Its cramped interior with two staggered seats was very clearly unsuitable for occupants suffering from claustrophobia. It carried two spare wheels. The 50-litre tank protruded into the passenger's foot room. At the rear there roared a Beetle engine with 985 cc capacity which the Porsche team had bumped up from the series-production 22 hp to 33 hp with enlarged intake valves, a sharper camshaft, increased compression and sporty down-draught carburettors. For a car weighing 525 kilograms, this engine performance produced a top speed of 160 km/h.

Porsche made three of this "Type 64", but the race never took place, as the Second World War broke out in September 1939. A Type 64 served as a fast courier car between Stuttgart and Carnatia for the design office – average speeds of 130 km/h were reported. Two cars survived the war, one of which, owned by the designer, was soon the first sports car to have the Porsche lettering on the front.

____ A Type 64, photographed in Gmünd in 1945. A mere 33 hp sufficed to propel this streamlined car at a top speed of 160 km/h.

79__ Porsche Type 360 Cisitalia

It's Hard to Shape the Future

Piero Dusio was a fast-moving industrialist from Turin. A designer of racing cars and amateur racing driver before the war, after it he was still rich enough to order a racing car from Porsche in Gmünd in February 1946.

Under the type number 360, Porsche created the future from light metal. The 180-degree V12 engine with 1.5 litres capacity delivered 300 hp at 8,000 rpm thanks to two Centric compressors. Power was supplied to the back wheels via sequential five-gear transmission with Porsche ring synchronisation, and front-wheel drive could be switched in. The space frame consisted of highly rigid steel, the bodywork of eye-wateringly expensive light-metal alloy. This work of art weighed about 720 kilograms. The first car was almost finished in November 1948. And Dusio was insolvent. Formula 1 is not cheap. Salvation was promised by the Argentinian dictator Juan Péron, who wanted to make fantastic cars in South America under the name "Autoar" with Dusio's assistance. Dusio sold his house, dismissed 400 employees and went to South America. The Type 360 followed in 1950 in the hold of a ship. When things had calmed down again at home, he returned to Italy without the Grand Prix car, produced textiles and tried his luck with less expensive automobiles.

In Argentina "Autoar" had meanwhile taken possession of the Type 360, as the company needed publicity. Somehow they got the prototype to work and measured 280 hp in the workshop. That seemed to be enough for an attempt on a world speed record, which was then broken, just, at 231 km/h. A second try in 1954 during a Formula Libre race failed. So the Type 360 remained in a garage in Buenos Aires until Porsche racing boss Huschke von Hanstein found it. Ferry Porsche bought this bird of paradise in 1959, and today the car can be admired in the Porsche Museum in Stuttgart.

____ The industrialist Piero Dusio (second from right) ordered the construction of this Grand Prix car from Porsche. Shortly after its presentation, Dusio disappeared to Argentina.

80__ Porsche Exclusive

Anything You Like

Ferry Porsche said " I started by looking around, but I couldn't find the car that I was dreaming of. So I decided to make it myself." Not everyone is a genius like Ferry, but at Porsche everyone can find his dream automobile. All it takes is plenty of money in the bank.

In the early years, the factory repair department took care of the racing exhaust for Sebring, and later a department for special wishes supplied dashboards made from burl wood. Since 1984 Porsche Exclusive has been reading its customers' minds. Discussions between clients and Exclusive can go on for days. Sometimes things happen quicker, as when an oil billionaire brought along his wife's handbag as a colour sample. Porsche Exclusive means: anything goes. Full leather furnishing, including the ventilation slats and all buttons, using eight cow hides, is a routine matter for Exclusive. It was more of a challenge to provide peacock paintwork in 18 colours or to make a revolver compartment with a spring mechanism in the central console. Or the 911 Turbo with a flat nose for a collector in New York. In 1990 40 people worked their way through his 28-page list of special wishes. And then there was the episode of the sheikh from Qatar. He put in an order for seven 959s. For each of them Porsche Exclusive developed a special paint with a matching interior of buffalo leather and an exhaust pipe gilded with 24-carat gold.

Sometimes Porsche Exclusive creates extremely small series. In 1993, in response to an inquiry, six 911 Turbo cabriolets, Type 964, were produced, and in 2012 enthusiasts could apply for delivery of one Porsche 911 Club out of the 13 that were made. In 2013 Porsche celebrated its five-millionth "Like" click on Facebook with a Facebook Edition. Porsche Exclusive made this one-off car after looking at the ideal configuration expressed by 54,000 fans. To love a car so much – that can easily make you jealous.

____ Porsche Exclusive makes everything possible, with Swabian meticulousness. Even the framing rings of the circular instruments are leather-covered.

RE PORSCHE

CLUSIVE

___ A sheikh from Qatar ordered seven Type 959 super sports cars all at once – each with unique special paintwork, and exhaust pipes made from 24-carat gold.

Porsche 9.

81__ Less is More

In Praise of What Makes You Tough

Pleasure at the simple, genuine things in life. It's hard to believe, but even for a luxury sports car like the 911 Turbo 3.3 Cabriolet in 1989, Porsche had a tempting offer for enthusiasts who wanted to get involved themselves. For 160,900 deutschmarks they could buy the 300-hp car with a manually operated canvas top. For a journey into a sudden summer thunderstorm, that meant either getting wet or stopping and fiddling about – the opportunity to enjoy a delicious little adventure, varying the routine of everyday managerial life. If desired, the Turbo could be bought for the same price with an electrically operated roof.

"Back to manual work" was also the motto in 2016 with the 911R, which Porsche, in an age of lightning-fast automatic gears, offered with a manual six-speed gearbox for nostalgic drivers. The 991 units of this 500-hp racer were sold out in advance at a price of 189,544 euros. Concentration on the authentic driving experience is also on offer in mega-hot machines such as, in 2015, the 911 GT3 RS: delivered without a radio and automatic air conditioning. You can guess why: a natural sound in natural surroundings, and a big weight-saving. Both radio and air conditioning are of course available at no extra cost for those who really do want to listen to something apart from the sound of the wonderful boxer engine.

Porsche literally scatters to the winds all we know about driving in draught-free conditions with the Speedster. The small windshield is a must, and it lets a magnificent hurricane into the cockpit as you drive. Only Porsche drivers who are also softies raise the wind blocker that is supplied with more recent models. Fewer frills means more enjoyment for all those who like to have their nose in the wind, especially when it is blowing hard. In an age of virtual reality, this feels like a luxury again.

____ Back to manual work. In 2016 the 911R was available with a conventional six-speed transmission. A wonderful piece of nostalgia that delighted the fans.

___ The original and the modern interpretation: on the right is the 911R, Porsche's first racing version of the model, dating from 1967–68, on the left the 911R road version of 2016.

MOMENTS

82___ Christophorus

Mrs Konnerth was the First Model

It is spring 1952, and Porsche has been producing sports cars in Stuttgart-Zuffenhausen for only two years. Marianne Konnerth is in the passenger seat of a 356 that Richard von Frankenberg is spiritedly and skilfully driving south. A wiry 30-year-old with dark horn-rimmed glasses and pomaded hair combed back in stream-lined form, he is a test and racing driver at Porsche, and at the same time a kind of early head of press relations, as well as the newly appointed editor-in-chief and author of "Christophorus", the "magazine for friends of the house of Porsche".

He had hatched the idea for the magazine back in 1950 with the graphic artist Erich Strenger, who was later to design legendary posters for Porsche. Now von Frankenberg, who chose the name of the patron saint of travellers for the future magazine, wanted to write a report about Swiss mountain roads. A story needs pictures, and pictures require a model. But Porsche had no money for models and preferred to adorn press photos of its sports cars with pictures of secretaries, which is how pretty Mrs Konnerth got her trip to Switzerland. She was married to a friend of von Frankenberg, and this was her first and only appearance as a model. On the Klausenpass the Munich photographer Heinz Hering took shots for the cover photo of the first "Christophorus", which appeared on 1 July 1952.

The magazine with articles about travel, personalities, exclusive background stories from Porsche development and racing was a brilliant success. From 1956 there were both German and English editions, and soon after that, "Christophorus" was published in three languages, six times a year. Now the three languages have become ten, the magazine appears five times annually, and its circulation has risen from 4,500 to 590,000.

___ The first issue of the customer magazine "Christophorus" appeared on 1 July 1952. Marianne Konnerth, an acquaintance of the editor-in-chief, acted as model for this cover photo on the Klausenpass.

Christophorus

ZEITSCHRIFT FÜR DIE FREUNDE
DES HAUSES PORSCHE

Nr. 1 / 1952

83__ The First Crash Test

Almost with a Living Dummy

It's the mid-sixties, and Porsche is rapidly growing as a manufacturer of highly coveted sports cars. There is the new 911, and the very exclusive 904 Carrera GTS, a mid-engine two-seater which is produced in small numbers. The USA quickly turns out to be the most important market – but at the same time difficult terrain, as passive safety is already a major issue on that side of the Atlantic. At Mercedes-Benz in Sindelfingen they have been crashing their cars in the interests of passenger safety since 1959. In Zuffenhausen they have occasionally bashed a Porsche 356 with weights, but that will be nowhere near enough to keep the Americans happy.

As so often in a small company, improvisation with some imagination and a slide rule was called for in the first crash tests. In 1965 a huge hydraulic crane came to Germany from the USA. Helmuth Bott, head of the experimental department, brought the monster to the factory yard in Zuffenhausen in 1966. An old 904 Carrera GTS was suspended from a glider coupling with its nose facing downwards. The technicians quickly calculated that, from a height of ten metres, the car would hit the ground at the required 50 km/h. The petrol tank under the front bonnet was filled with water.

A particularly daring employee came up with the idea of having himself fastened inside the 904 Carrera GTS and plummeting downwards as a crash-test dummy. This man was Rolf Wütherich – the top mechanic who was sitting next to James Dean in September 1955 when the actor had his fatal accident in a Porsche 550 Spyder. Well-meaning colleagues persuaded Wütherich to abandon his plan, and the car fell empty to the ground. The first big crash test in the history of Porsche was completed without injury. Today Porsche has one of the world's most modern crash facilities in Weissach.

____ Home-made crash test: for lack of elaborate crash-testing facilities, Porsche dropped a 904 Carrera GTS from a crane from a height of ten metres.

84__ Type Numbers

The 911 Is Not the 911th

Everything was simpler in the old days. Life was simpler, there was a choice between two TV channels – and the identification of Porsche models was easy to understand. Every project had a type number, and that was that.

Admittedly, old Ferdinand cheated and gave his first job the number 7 so it would not seem to be a first try. But after that, he counted properly. 22 was the Auto Union GP racing car, 60 the Beetle. 356 was the first sports car, and now take note: the type number became the name of the model. For the successor to the 356, Porsche departed from strict numerical order. Cooperative ventures with Volkswagen were in the offing. At VW in Wolfsburg the development jobs also had three-digit numbers, and 9 had not been used. And so the successor to the 356 got the type number 901. From now on it was less about counting and more a matter of making sure that the type numbers were clearly distinct. 914 for the mid-engine car, 924 for the first transaxle Porsche, then 928 for the big Gran Turismo. The "4" at the end stood for four cylinders, the "8" for double that number of cylinders. With the 911 something happened that marketing people dream of: even after seven generations of sports cars, this number marks a rear-wheel drive with an unmistakeable silhouette.

Internally Porsche allocates each generation and each special 911 its own type number. The first 911 Turbo was the 930, the first with four-wheel drive was the 953. Then it got more complicated, as from 1993 the sports cars were given names – and internal numbers: Carrera GT (980), Boxster (986), Cayenne (955). In 2016 Porsche simplified the names and numbers in a new system: two-door models got a number, with the Boxster and Cayman having the legendary 718 for mid-engine cars. Four-door models, by contrast, were known in public only by their names. It's as easy as that.

____ 901 was the original type number of the 911. Though this rear-wheel-drive car was neither the 901st nor the 911th that Porsche designed. A complicated story …

großen Viersitzer!", und alle Jahre wieder mußten wir diese Meldungen dementieren— auch in diesem Jahr! Porsche brachte keinen neuen, großen viersitzigen Wagen zur Ausstellung, aber:

Seit Jahren haben sich Ferry Porsche und sein Ingenieurstab den Kopf darüber zerbrochen, wie das Porsche-Leitmotiv „Fahren in seiner schönsten Form" up-to-date gehalten und den ständig wechselnden Bedingungen des modernen Verkehrs angepaßt werden kann. Denn was heißt schon „Fahren in seiner schönsten Form?" Versteht nicht jeder von uns darunter etwas anderes? Hat nicht ein Geschäftsmann, der jeden Morgen von seinem Hause am Stadtrand in Kolonne zu seinem Büro fährt, oder die Dame, die einige Stunden später beim Shopping verzweifelt nach einem Platz an einem groschenhungrigen Parkometer sucht, ganz andere Vorstellungen vom „Fahren in seiner schönsten Form" als die kinderreiche Familie, die an die Nordsee auf Urlaub fährt, oder das glückliche junge Paar, das in einem offenen Zweisitzer auf der Autostrada del Sole mit hoher Reisegeschwindigkeit und wenig Gepäck der Sonne Süditaliens entgegenfährt?

Der Geschäftsmann wird sich für sein meterweises Vorwärtskriechen sicher einen großen Amerikaner mit automatischer Kupplung wünschen; die Dame beim Parken von einem der bisher nur auf dem Papier existenten Stadtwagen träumen; der Familienvater Wert auf mindestens sechs komfortable Plätze legen und das junge Paar mit einem spartanisch ausgerüsteten Sportwagen vorlieb nehmen, wenn es sich nur den südlichen Wind bei hoher Geschwindigkeit um die Nase wehen lassen kann: dies sind nur vier Beispiele von den unzähligen Vorstellungen, die ebenso unzählige Autokäufer von dem haben, was für sie und ihre speziellen Bedürfnisse und Wünsche „Fahren in seiner schönsten Form" bedeutet.

Wie sieht es bei uns Porschefahrern aus?

Die Porsche-Ingenieure waren die ersten, die vor über 10 Jahren begannen, ein sportliches und zugleich bequemes Reisefahrzeug in größerer Serie zu bauen. Das beste Pferd im Stalle ist heute der Carrera 2000 GS; — ein Beweis dafür, daß in Zuffenhausen der einmal eingeschlagene Weg konsequent fortgesetzt

85__ Across the Atlantic

In 1950 Porsche Started up in the USA

For over 60 years the USA was Porsche's biggest and most important market, regularly supplied from Zuffen-hausen with half of all the sports cars built there. Impulses for Porsche icons came from the USA: the Speedster, Targa, Turbo, 928. When the American economy went downhill after the stock-exchange crash in 1987, Porsche almost went the same way. However, nowhere is there more enthusiasm for the brand – the Porsche Club of America has 117,300 members and is the world's biggest marque club.

It all began in October 1950, when Max Hoffman put Porsche 356s in his showroom on Park Avenue, at the corner of 55th Street in Manhattan. Hoffman, an Austrian who had emigrated in 1938, sold European luxury cars here. A few weeks earlier at the Auto-Salon in Paris he and Ferdinand Porsche had decided to make Americans acquainted with the zippy German cars. "Maxie" was a brilliant salesman: he proposed to Ferry Porsche that the cars should have a coat of arms. Because every car in the USA had one – Porsche, too, from 1954. The Speedster, Hoffman's idea, made the breakthrough in America. While Hoffman worked the East Coast, his friend Johnny von Neumann was active on the West Coast, taking the 356 to film stars.

Sales boomed, but customer service lagged behind. In 1952 Porsche had therefore sent Herbert Linge to train mechanics. Wolfgang Raether put things right with dealers and customer service, and was succeeded in October 1955 by the north German Otto-Erich Filius. Filius founded the Porsche of America Corporation, Porsche's own network for sales and customer service. Hoffman left the business in 1963 with a golden handshake: 150 dollars for every Porsche sold in the USA until the total reached a million. Over the decades, the Corporation became Porsche Cars North America (PCNA), the biggest Porsche organisation outside Germany.

___ It's 1959, and the first Porsches are being shipped across the Atlantic to the USA, which quickly became the biggest market for the marque.

86__ Far, Far Away

The First Porsches in Australia

In summer 1951 on the Grossglockner Pass, Norman Hamilton was urging his Oldsmobile uphill. A pump manufacturer from Melbourne, he had come to Austria to see the latest European technology on reservoir dams. What he then saw, though, was something low-slung and silver that whizzed past his Olds. A little further on, the small sports car was standing by the roadside. Hamilton greeted the driver, who introduced himself as Richard von Frankenberg, press relations man and racing driver for Porsche.

The two men got along well straight away, and Frankenberg presented Hamilton to Ferry Porsche. They shook hands on their agreement to make Hamilton the Porsche importer for Australia. He ordered a fish-silver 356 cabriolet and a chestnut-brown coupé. Porsche produced the cabriolet with right-wheel drive – a first for the 356. With his friend Andrew Kennedy, Hamilton picked the cars up from the factory on 6 September 1951. They drove their precious automobiles to Genoa, where the Porsches disappeared into the hold of the SS Australia. On 1 November Hamilton presented the two 356s to sports-car lovers in Melbourne. One of them said: "For most of us, the Porsche was a collection of exotic parts." Motor sports is good advertising, thought Hamilton, and took part in races and rallies. Soon he had sold the cabriolet, but the coupé faced an ordeal: a 10,400-kilometre race right around Australia in August 1953. He strapped an extra tank to the roof rack and drilled two holes in the bonnet at the front. Through one of them Hamilton threaded a petrol tube from the roof tank, while the other was used to attach an additional headlight. The 356 patiently endured all of this, survived a collision with a kangaroo, and finished 14th.

Both Porsches disappeared for decades, until two collectors in Melbourne tracked them down, and they are now on the road there, pristine and priceless.

____ On November 1951 the first right-wheel-drive Porsche came to the showroom in Melbourne, Australia. "A collection of exotic parts", said the Aussies.

87__ The 1965 Monte Carlo Rally

"It's Fine if You Finish Last."

In January 1965, four months after production of the 911 started, Huschke von Hanstein, head of press relations, had the idea to present this sports car to the wealthy little country on the Côte d'Azur, and especially to its prince. Master mechanic Herbert Linge and test engineer Peter Falk were given the task of driving down in one of the 13 prototypes. They were to do this in the context of the world-famous Monte Carlo Rally. "But for heaven's sake, don't scratch it", were the instructions. "It's fine if you finish last", were von Hanstein's parting words to his rally team.

Linge, however, was a racing driver through and through, and Falk had already gained tens of thousands of kilometres of experience as a co-driver in rallies. As Falk later recalled, "As soon as we were in the car, one thing was clear: we would drive fast. No hanging around, that's not why we were there." The 911 had a lovingly assembled two-litre engine with approximately 150 hp, the gearing ratio was shorter, and the locking differential ensured better traction, even in slippery conditions. To the usual rally accessories such as a roll-over bar, bucket seats, a reading lamp and a precise distance meter, Linge and Falk had added a tube. Into this tube Falk shouted the details of the route recorded in training. The tube ended at Linge's right ear – an archaic but remarkably reliable intercom that worked superbly.

The 1965 Monte Carlo Rally was one of the snowiest and most chaotic in its history. 237 teams set off, but only 24 made it to the finish in Monaco over icy roads and through snow drifts and blizzards. A Porsche 904 took second place. The red 911 with number 147 managed a sensational fifth place, and on 25th January Prince Rainier set eyes on the 911 for the first time – with no scratches in the paintwork.

___ The Monte Carlo Rally in 1965, with Herbert Linge at the wheel and Peter Falk in the passenger seat. Planned as a delivery to Prince Rainier, the drive ended with fifth place in a tough rally.

Departing for the
Monte Carlo Rally in
1965: driver Herbert Linge
(right), co-driver
Peter Falk with a 911;
driver Eugen Böhringer
(in the car) and
Rolf Wütherich (left) with
a 904 Carrera GTS.

88__Monza, 4 November 1967

All Broken – the Car and Five World Records

Monza, 29 October 1967, 12 noon. A Porsche 906 racing car leaves the pits. The drivers Jo Siffert, Dieter Spörry, Rico Steinemann and Charles Vögele have their eyes on world records. Four days of driving lie ahead: they aim to be the world's fastest over 15,000 kilometres, 10,000 miles, 20,000 kilometres, 72 hours and 96 hours.

Ten hours later, the front axle was ripped from its frame. The g-forcess in the banked curves, the terrible track surface and the weight of spare parts that had to be in the car to comply with regulations were too much. Yet there was still hope: if they continued within 48 hours, any new records would stand. So on Monday at 7 am, the phone rang at Porsche: "Help!" Three hours later an emergency plan had been made: two 911Rs – the racing version of the 911 – were as good as ready for action. One would break the records, the other would drive to Monza as a spare-parts store. Two fifth gears had been installed in the record-breaker, as it was not clear if the teeth of the fifth gear would stand 20,000 kilometres of maximum stress.

Soon the rapid spare-parts store was on the road. At 6 pm the driver phoned from the Swiss border: the customs officers would not let him pass, as the 911R was too noisy. Instead he drove to Turin and Monza via France. An hour later the record-breaker car was also on its way, heading through Austria to Italy, where the throatiness of the racing engine brought tears of joy to the customs officers' eyes. Early on Tuesday, the two 911Rs were in Monza, the spare parts packed in the car for the record attempt, restarting at 8 pm. The weather was dreadful. Additional tread was cut into the racing tyres, and the carburettors iced up once. Nevertheless, on Saturday, 4 November, at 8 pm, all the records had been broken: 96 hours at 208.3 km/h.

___ November 1967: the 911R has to survive 24 hours of flat-out driving for a world-record attempt at Monza. The mechanics are checking all important functions during a change of driver.

89__ Porsche 917

Eureka! – Thanks to Dead Flies

In 1969 the Porsche 917 was a young racing car, but it already had a very bad reputation. Initiated by Ferdinand Piëch to make Porsche invincible in endurance races, the streamlined, low-slung racer with 560 hp and a top speed over 350 km/h was considered almost impossible to handle. When the season ended Porsche went to the Österreichring in Austria in October for tests in order to exorcise the demons in the 12-cylinder beast. But neither the Porsche engineers nor the technicians of the British partner team JWA could find a solution. Until the flies died.

The engineer Helmut Flegl, responsible for the 917 at Porsche, had brought along vertical rear spoilers. They produced some downforce, and above all a eureka moment. Flegl, his boss Peter Falk and John Horsman from JWA noticed that, after a few laps, dead flies were sticking just below the upper edge of the spoiler, whereas the rest was clean. They rapidly drew the right conclusion: the air stream above the downward-sloping tail was only flowing to the upper edge of the spoiler. So the rear had to be given a different shape: it would have to rise at the back like a wedge. A new wedge tail was quickly improvised from sheet aluminium, and hey presto: the 917 was more stable, the lap times were faster.

One tricky task remained: Piëch was visiting the tests. He had to be told of the demise of the bodywork that he had radically cut down to get low air resistance. Falk picked him up from the airstrip and started by explaining that the 917 was now five seconds faster. Then he gave him the news about the wedge-shaped tail. Piëch was annoyed, and walked in silence around the car in the pits. Thunder was in the air. Then he asked the drivers. Brian Redman and Leo Kinnunen reported miracles. At that, everything was fine for the thoroughbred engineer Piëch. And from then onwards, the 917 won everything that could be won.

____ That's the solution: on the Österreichring the technicians improvised a wedge-shaped tail for the 917 – which then had much improved road-holding.

90__ Le Mans 1970

Wearing the Crown

4 June 1970, 4 pm: Porsche has won the 24 Hours of Le Mans for the first time. Hans Herrmann and the British driver Richard Attwood triumphed in the red-and-white, short-tailed Porsche 917 from Porsche Salzburg, with the number 23 – Herrmann's lucky number and his birthday, 23 February 1928. After narrowly losing in the previous year, the Swabian driver enjoyed a wonderful triumph – and retired from racing. He had made this promise to his wife when he left for France. For Attwood, too, this victory put everything to rights. In 1969, driving a 917 with Vic Elford, he had led by no less than six laps, almost 80 kilometres, when the clutch failed.

It was a hard-fought first victory for Porsche. Seven Porsche 917s started, and the main opposition was Ferrari, with eleven Type 512S entered for the race. Soon rain was falling, then it was pouring down, and following a mass collision after almost three hours the four fastest Ferraris were out of the race. Today it is inconceivable to manoeuvre a Porsche 917 with 580 hp and a weight of 800 kilograms flat out round a watery Le Mans circuit. After ten hours, number 23 took the lead. And stayed there. When the chequered flag came out, only seven out of 52 cars that had started were still in the classification. Herrmann and Attwood aquaplaned their Porsche round the course at an average speed of about 191 km/h. The only traction control was in their heads and their feet. The fact that two further Porsche teams were on the podium consummated the triumph.

A year earlier Porsche and its head of sports, the Austrian visionary Ferdinand Piëch, had achieved a goal that had been thought unattainable: in 1969 they won the world championship, led by Piëch, and with the 917 they repeated the feat in 1970. But the crowning glory in endurance racing was and still is awarded in the Département Sarthe.

____ The Porsche 917 in the rain – as it was in 1970 in Le Mans. With a sensitive foot on the accelerator, Hans Herrmann and Dick Attwood drove their red-and-white Porsche to victory.

___ Le Mans, 1970: in weather like this, today the race would proceed behind the safety car at reduced speed. Back in those days, the cars drove full throttle with 580 hp through the water.

91__ 1,000 Kilometres of Spa-Francorchamps 1971

Four Tenths of a Second

The 1,000-kilometres race on the road circuit at Spa-Francorchamps in the Belgian Ardennes on 9 May 1971 got under everyone's skin – and on a team boss's nerves. First of all the British driver Derek Bell did the fastest practice lap of all time in a short-tail 917. In 3 minutes 14.6 seconds his 600-hp Porsche ate up the 14.1 kilometres of closed-off country roads. His average speed was 260.8 km/h. In the race, Bell took turns at the wheel with the Swiss driver Jo Siffert. Their team colleagues and greatest rivals were the Mexican Pedro Rodriguez and the Englishman Jackie Oliver. Shortly after the start, in drizzly conditions, Siffert and Rodriguez got away from the field and took off into in a different universe. Their Porsches lapped the whole field. At insane speeds they flew into the bends, one car next to the other. Their 917s touched in a no-holds-barred fight. Following the change of drivers Bell chased Oliver mercilessly round the track in the final laps.

This was too much for the team boss. He showed a signal to the combatants: "Keep your positions". The man holding the sign leaned over the wall in the pit lane. 50 metres away, Siffert was urging Bell on: "Go for it, put your foot on the gas, get him!" Bell seemed to be doing just that and drove part of the last lap next to Oliver. Then the two Porsches shot over the finishing line like aircraft flying in diagonal formation. Rodriguez/Oliver beat Siffert/Bell by four tenths of a second after the fastest road race in history. The winners' time was four hours, one minute and 9.7 seconds at an average of 249.069 km/h – including pit stops. Tragic events showed how dangerous this sport was: neither Rodriguez nor Siffert was alive at the end of the year. The Mexican died in a Ferrari at a sports-car race in Nuremberg. The Swiss driver lost his life in a BRM Formula 1 at Brands Hatch in England.

___ Two Porsche 917s in close combat at Spa in 1971. After 1,000 kilometres, car no. 21 won with a lead of 0.4 seconds. The winner's average speed was 249 km/h.

From May 1998 Porsche
offered this 911 GT1 for sale.
The first mid-engine 911,
a basis for racing cars, cost
1.55 million deutschmarks.

SUPER SPORTS CARS

92__ Porsche 959

What Is Possible in Sports Car Design?

Everyone who loves sports cars knows the Porsche 959 and can recite its technical data by heart. What Porsche produced here from 1986 to 1988 was fascination with the automobile in its purest form. A highly streamlined 911 with an engine derived from the unbeatable 962C racing car. Engine displacement 2.85 litres, staged turbo charging through two turbos that gave propulsion like a Saturn V, even from low revs. 450 hp in the "tame" version, which took almost four seconds to sprint to 100 km/h. 515 hp for the 959 Sport, which was 100 kilograms lighter, a great deal harder and therefore not recommended for people with false teeth. This machine could reach a top speed of 339 km/h according to "auto motor and sport".

But in developing it, Porsche was more interested in high-tech than in high speed alone. What was possible in sports-car design? The answer: an early smart four-wheel drive with ABS, four pre-settable shock-absorber programmes, automatic and speed-dependent height adjustment, bodywork with an intelligent mix of materials (aluminium, sheet steel and plastic), tyre-pressure control and heaven knows what else. The idea was to win the world rally championship with the 959, but the plan had to be abandoned when the high-tech turbo beasts were banned following severe accidents. So Porsche set out on the 14,000-kilometre Paris–Dakar marathon through the Sahara with the high-tech car. It won at the second attempt, in 1986.

292 of them were sold at a price of 420,000 deutschmarks to the usual suspects, customers such as Herbert von Karajan, Bill Gates, Boris Becker and Don Johnson. The company made no profit with the 959, as development and production were too expensive. Helmuth Bott, head of development, described the 959 as the most expensive advertising give-away in Porsche's history. But it did a lot to put a shine on the company's image.

____ With the 959, Porsche put future technology on the road in the late 1980s. A 2,85-litre double-turbo engine catapulted this high-tech machine to more than 300 km/h.

In 1986 this was the ultimate
Porsche: the 959 with smart
four-wheel drive and 450 hp in
the tame version. For extremists,
the Sport version had 515 hp.

93__ Porsche 911 GT1 Road

The First Mid-Engine 911

This super sports car owed its existence to a paragraph in the rule book of the Gran Turismo world championship in 1996. In order to take part, Porsche had to show that there were at least 25 roadworthy examples of the sports car. Between 1996 and 1998 the racing department constructed 23 "911 GT1 Road" cars – significantly more than competitors put on the road – and the sports officials gave the go-ahead.

From May 1998 Porsche put the GT1 on sale for the extraordinary price of 1,550,000 deutschmarks, and these rare birds sold out immediately. What the customers got for their money was the first 911 with a mid-engine. This position enables a better weight distribution for racing and a big tail diffusor, i.e. an aerodynamic aid that sucks the back of the car down onto the road surface by means of low air pressure. The engine was the first water-cooled six-cylinder boxer with a four-valve cylinder head that Porsche had put on the road. Thanks to a twin turbo, this 3.2-litre powerhouse generated 544 hp and 600 Newton metres. This was passed to the rear axle via a six-speed manual transmission. The racing engine must have been severely under-challenged in road traffic, just like the enormous carbon brake disks with a diameter of almost 40 centimetres and eight-piston brake callipers on the front axle (at the back: four pistons). For the chassis Porsche opted for a mixed construction of sheet steel for the front and a space frame for the rear end, with a cover of carbon-Kevlar plastic. With a kerb weight of only 1,150 kilograms, the 911 GT1 hurtled from zero to 100 km/h in 3.7 seconds. After 10.5 seconds it reached 200, and the top speed was 310 kilometres per hour. With its width of 1.98 metres, good judgement was needed in passing narrow highway road works, and the height of 1.10 metres is a hint that GT1 owners needed flexible legs and hips for getting in and out.

____ A rare version of that inexhaustible theme, the 911. 23 examples were built of the 911 GT1 Road. The air inlet on the roof leads to the intercooler.

94_ Porsche Carrera GT

The Last of the Old School

First of all the background: for the 24 Hours of Le Mans in 2000, Porsche conceived a wonderful V10 racing engine. But after 16 overall wins, Porsche boss Wiedeking was no longer convinced of the value of a 17th victory. His idea was to make a second super sports car, following the 959, and the V10 powerhouse would drive this Über-Porsche. This would give Ferrari, McLaren and Bugatti a rival as a road racing car that worked reliably, didn't have to be pampered, could handle a traffic jam on the way to the office and was devilishly fast.

No sooner said than done. The 5.7-litre V10 was tamed at 612 hp with 8,900 wonderful-sounding revs. For the chassis consisting of 1,000 carbon-fibre, magnesium and aluminium parts, Porsche developed several processes. The car later registered 70 new patents. It goes without saying that records tumbled during the tests on the Nürburgring with Walter Röhrl. The presentation of the Carrera GT on 28 September 2000 on the Champs-Élysées was a quite different challenge for Röhrl: the pre-series-production car still had a rough racing engine, the throttle was stiff and hard to adjust – highly delicate conditions for a low-speed drive to the Louvre in pouring rain.

From 2003 the Carrera GT was on sale at 452,400 euros. For a driving presentation for international media, Porsche decided on a former Soviet airfield, Gross Dölln near Berlin. The runway was 4,500 metres long, which sufficed to reach a speed of 330 km/h. 200 km/h were reached after 9.9 seconds in third gear. The driver switched into fourth at 235, into fifth gear at 280 km/h. Porsche dispensed with fashionable gimmicks such as gearshift paddles, an adjustable chassis or launch control. The Carrera GT is an old-style machine, guaranteed to be without artificial additives and softeners. Jay Leno called it "the last old-school super sports car."

___ Porsche registered 70 patents for the Carrera GT. The engineer's art in concentrated form, it brought the fascination of racing to the roads and was presented by Porsche on a runway for jet aircraft.

A master moving
sideways: Walter Röhrl
in a Carrera GT
demonstrating
"power oversteering"
with the skid control
turned off. Not for
the uninitiated.

95___ Porsche 918 Spyder

The One with Three Hearts

The 918 Spyder: where should we start the list of superlatives? Porsche's first plug-in hybrid had no less than three engines. An electric motor on the front axle generated 129 hp; the e-motor at the back added 156 hp; and then there were 608 hp from the 4.6-litre V8. A system total of 893 hp – more than any road Porsche ever had. "Wonderful" was the first reaction of the public at the automobile salon in Geneva in spring 2010.

The decision was quickly taken to make 918 of these cars, and on 18.9.2013 (9/18 as written in the USA) the artists in the Zuffenhausen factory went to work. Two weeks earlier the Porsche engineer and works driver Marc Lieb had scorched a superlative into the surface of the North Loop at the Nürburgring: 6:57 minutes! No sports car authorised to drive on public roads had ever managed that. The order books were full. The price of 768,025 euros seemed reasonable to the well-heeled global clientele. Some of them even forked out 71,600 euros extra for the Weissach package with more carbon fibre and 41 kilograms less weight. For their money the customers got a concentrated dose of automotive high-tech. A carbon-fibre chassis wrapped in a carbon-fibre skin. The triple engines accelerate the 1,634-kilo car to 100 km/h in 2.6 seconds, to 200 in 7.3 seconds of bliss. When the brakes are applied, the electric motors act as generators to recharge the liquid-cooled lithium-ion battery. A package of electronics distils the interaction of the engines in five selectable modes with the differential lock, the rear-axle steering, the shock absorbers, the wings, spoilers and air vents to make irresistible driving dynamics, underscored by the sound of two exhaust pipes as thick as a man's arm on the top of the V8. On 19 June 2015, 918 Spyders had been manufactured.

___ The 918 Spyder is Porsche's latest word on the super sports car – and the most powerful so far, with 893 hp. The hybrid powering of this two-seater is an exploration of the future.

____ Taycan is the first fully electric Porsche sports car. This silent racer was released in 2020 – 120 years after Ferdinand Porsche's first e-mobile.

PROTOTYPES

96__A 911 for Four:

Far from Easy

A sports car with four full-sized seats. This idea had been on Ferry Porsche's mind for a long time already when the 911 had its premiere in September 1963. The blessed Porsche 356 had existed in a zippy limousine version, the 530, in 1952, but did not go into series production. In 1959–60 Ferdinand Alexander Porsche then designed the 754 T7, which admittedly had space for two very slim passengers in the back beneath its pagoda-like roof, but with the standard engines it failed to provide enough luggage space for four. It remained a prototype.

In 1969 a second attempt was made. Under design number 915 the Italian studio Pininfarina proposed a B17 with a horizontal roof and a steeply sloping back window. Neither the shape nor the handling of the model, a 911 lengthened by 20 centimetres, impressed the test drivers. Nor did the rival in-house design called the C20 get further than the prototype stage: it was too expensive and not really a Porsche sports car. In 1988 the board approved the "989" project. Business was not good, and the aim was to expand the customer base. The 989 was a four-door vehicle with a 300-hp 3.6-litre V8 front engine, rear-wheel drive and a wheelbase that had been extended a good 55 centimetres beyond that of the 2+2-seater. At 5.9 seconds from zero to 100 and a top speed of 270 km/h, it sounded very much like a Porsche. Yet the board members may not have had a distinct view of the extremely good-looking prototype, as the development costs put tears in their eyes. 600 million deutschmarks, it was reported, and by the time production started in the mid-90s that sum would probably have risen to a billion. In order to make money with the 989, Zuffenhausen would have had to double the target selling price of 80,000 marks. The supervisory board stopped the 989 project in January 1991. What a pity!

____ A 911 to seat four was intended to look like this. The front of the prototype found favour, but the rear and the idea of a proper four-seater were rejected.

97__ Porsche 928 H50

Porsche's First Four-Door GT

The Porsche 928 was a wonderful Gran Turismo. Its water-cooled V8 mobilised a decent amount of power. Thanks to its transaxle construction with a front engine and gearbox in front of the rear axle, the car's balance was excellent, and the light-metal suspension was one of the best that could be had at the time. But unfortunately, fans of the 928 endured the same experience as 911 enthusiasts: the back seats were only suitable for small children, masochists or yogis.

In a technical exercise in 1984, the workforce made a genuine four-seater 928 for their boss Ferry for his 75th birthday. However, this 928-4 remained a one-off, much used by Ferry. In 1987 Porsche tackled the lack of space with a view to series production, and designed two prototypes with a longer wheelbase and four full-sized seats: project 928 H50. Indeed, two large armchair seats in the back were an invitation to take a comfortable, earth-bound journey at the speed of a sporting aircraft. The engine had grown meanwhile to 4.9 litres capacity and generated 320 horsepower, which sufficed for a top speed of 270 km/h. Fitted out entirely in leather, with a high-end sound system and automatic air-conditioning, it pampered the driver and passengers in late 1980s style. The big attraction of the H50 was its four doors, the rear ones attached to the C pillar. The B pillar was absent, which greatly facilitated getting into the back seats.

The feature that provided the comfort also put an end to the project. After about 8,000 test kilometres, the chassis was judged to be too soft. An H50 was given to the partner company ASC, with whom Porsche had built the prototype. The other H50 disappeared into a hangar, turned up again in 2012 at an auto show in Pebble Beach in California, and can be admired today in the Porsche Museum in Stuttgart.

____ The prototype of the 928 H50, with a longer wheelbase, four full seats and no B pillar – the rear doors were attached to the C pillar. Only two were made.

98___ Porsche 965

"It Feels Very Safe at 300."

It almost became reality: in the late 1980s a new top model was conceived as the crowning glory of the 911 series. The project, which was given the type number 965, got the go-ahead in 1984. The formal vocabulary of the Type 965 took its cue from the flat headlights and integrated rear wing of the 959 super sports car – a citation that was no empty promise.

The prototypes made a good impression, even on experienced test drivers – on the Mont Ventoux downhill run, for example. They reported that the 1,435-kilogram car was easier to handle than the 959, but definitely had enough power. On the high-speed test ground at Nardo in Italy in autumn 1988, the car reached 300 km/h without any difficulty, with a 3.4-litre twin-turbo engine and approximately 350 hp. For the engine, Porsche considered a number of alternatives, from the water-cooled six-cylinder boxer to a four-valve V8 that had been derived from a racing engine for the American Indy series. The electronically regulated four-wheel drive, the automatic ride height adjustment and the refined aerodynamics immediately conveyed "a very safe feeling", even at 300 km/h. If desired, the 965 could be fitted with the lightning-fast Porsche PDK double clutch.

When the head of development, Helmuth Bott, retired at the end of 1988, his successor Ulrich Bez stopped work on the 965 as soon as he took office. The reasons for this were rising development costs and a change in the company's model strategy. Today only a single prototype remains. The matte-black "Black Bomber", as the car was christened in Weissach, conceals under its rear hood a large-volume Audi V8 engine that was fitted for the purpose of radiator tests. This one-off car can be admired in the Porsche Museum from time to time.

___ A model of the Porsche 965 in the secret design studio of Porsche Style. Unfortunately the project for a new top-end 911 came to nothing.

99___Porsche 984

An Entry-Level Two-Seater

How many concept studies, test vehicles and prototypes see the light of day and then fall victim unseen to the "delete" button, paper shredder or metal press? Few people know, even at the company sites in Weissach, Zuffenhausen and Leipzig. The 984 did at least reach the prototype stage, and one specimen survives in the Porsche Museum in Stuttgart-Zuffenhausen.

Between 1984 and 1987 Porsche worked on this handy, light, not especially expensive roadster, positioned as the first Porsche for younger customers and known internally as the "Junior". And it has to be said: this would have been a fine thing! In the best Porsche tradition, the aim was a zippy performance with relatively modest fuel consumption by means of low weight and excellent aerodynamics. Parts of the bodywork consisted of plastic reinforced with glass fibre. Plexiglas side windows were not wound up and down but fixed, and reminiscent of icons such as the Speedster. An air-cooled boxer engine with 120 to 150 hp was to take up the classic rear position. The steel box-section frame proved to have high rigidity from the very start. Rear wheel drive (though initially 4WD was considered), a drivetrain with double transverse control arms, and brakes from the 911 promised to deliver superb handling. A tilting roof cover of hard plastic, futuristic at the time, put the icing on this tasty-looking cake.

On 31 July 1987 the prototype had its first outing on the country roads around Weissach. On 15 February 1988 the roadster's comfort was tested. However, at this time the sharp fall of the dollar was making a deep dent in sales figures. Instead of designing new models, a way out of the sales crisis was suddenly called for. So farewell, roadster! Yet it returned, more beautiful than ever. In 1993 at the motor show in Detroit a compact two-seater called a Boxster was displayed on the Porsche stand.

___ A dream for young Porsche fans. The Type 984 was developed as a relatively low-price entry-level sports car, but the project was terminated in 1988.

100__ Porsche Taycan

Yes! It's goose bumps!

So Porsche has come full circle. It all began in 1900 with young Ferdinand Porsche's "Lohner Porsche Electro-mobile", driven by electric motors with 1.8 kW (2.5 hp) at each front wheel. The four-seater was capable of up to 35 kph, with an action range of 50 kilometres at best. With the Taycan things are a little different.

Porsche unveiled their first fully electric sports car on 4 September, 2019, draped with data that made sports car aficionados stop in their tracks. 0 to 100 km/h in less than three seconds. An electric machine at the front and another at the rear axle generate 625 hp (overboost: 761 hp for 2.5 secs) in the top of the range "Turbo S" (yes, "Turbo" still stands for utmost grunt). Maximum speed is 260 km/h and torque peaks at a whopping 1,050 New-tonmetres. One might recall the mighty 917/30 Turbo, when 1,000 Newtons of torque took our breath away.

Speaking of the old days, until the early 80s Porsche tested their brakes racing down Mont Ventoux in Southern France. 21 steep, windy kilometres, full bore. For the Taycan´s acceleration tests, Porsche applied the same all-out principle. A Taycan prototype did 26 sprints from standstill to 200 kph (in under 10 secs), consecutively. No down-time for the batteries. No problem. That's Porsche for you. What else is important for a sports car? Weight: almost 2.3 tons. But boy, they go nimbly around the corners thanks to the lowest centre of gravity of all Porsche road cars, a good weight distribution and torque vectoring, which works like very clever self-locking diffs. Sure, there's some work here for Weissach until we can do a splash and dash, but 25 minutes for up to 80% recharge is the best you can get with an e-car and allows time to settle the adrenaline. But then: 16,000 revs! The times when you got goose bumps from 4,000 upwards are gone. But there's this power-hum like a space-ship picking up speed in old sci-fi movies. Combined with that crazy acceleration it just gives you that special feeling … yes! It's goose bumps!

___ The Taycan retains the Porsche design DNA with the roofline sloping downward to the rear, the sleek cabin and drawn-in rear C-pillar, and the pronounced shoulders of the wings. The 911 sends its best regards!

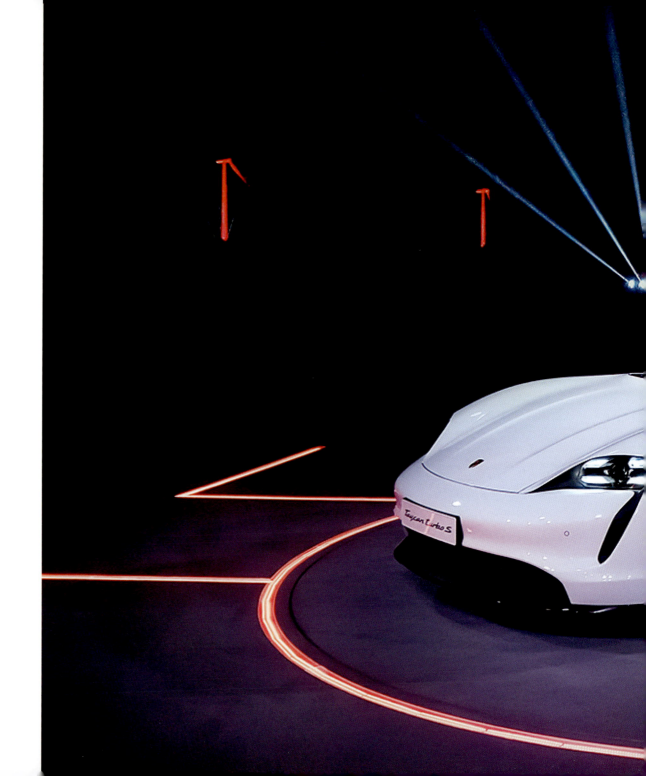

Porsche unveiled the Taycan on 4 September, 2019 near a wind farm on China's Pingtan Island (picture), at the Niagara Falls representing water power and at a solar farm close to Berlin.

Two Porsche 914/6s in the steeply banked curves at Daytona. This racing track in Florida is one of the world's most renowned, and Porsche holds the record for victories here.

THE MOST AMAZING TRACKS

101___24 Hours of Daytona

A Long Night in Florida

The 24 Hours of Daytona is a different kettle of fish from the 24 Hours of Le Mans. The race in Florida takes place in January, so the days are short and the nights very long, dark and cold – a contrast to summer in France. The Daytona International Speedway is not even half as long as the Circuit des 24 Heures. Yet at least as many entrants jostle on the 5.729 kilometres of track, which means things are crowded and hectic.

Usually the Speedway is a typically American oval: three banked corners connected by straights. But at the 24 Hours, the racing cars whizz through only two banked curves and then turn off into the twisty infield. At Daytona the teams are confronted by strange challenges: how do I tune a car so that it doesn't bottom out in the banked curves yet can still be driven properly in the infield? How do I improvise my little workshop on the pit lane? In Daytona there are no permanent pits, as at Le Mans. Another contrast to Le Mans, where it is quiet in the pits at times when the cars disappear into the woods on the 13.5-kilometre circuit, in Daytona the noise never ceases for 24 hours – a factor that makes high demands on the nerves of the pit teams.

The speedway track was opened in 1959, and in 1966 the first 24-hour race was held. Hans Herrmann and Herbert Linge brought a in a Porsche 906 home in sixth place. Three years later Porsche celebrated a triple triumph. Vic Elford and Jochen Neerpasch drove the victorious 907, and press boss Huschke von Hanstein also briefly put Stommelen, Siffert and Herrmann into the cockpit, which means that all of them are recorded in the chronicles as winners. Until today Porsche has amassed 22 overall wins at Daytona. Stuttgart holds the record – so there is, after all, something that Le Mans and Daytona have in common.

___ This is Daytona: a banked curve in the background, and the Porsche 907 that won in 1968 is already in the twisty infield, where fans camp on the grass.

___ Four Porsche 907s in the pits in Daytona in 1968. The barrels on stilts are for refuelling, and in the night the mechanics shivered in a cold wind.

102___ Sebring International Raceway

"Twice as Painful"

The 12 Hours of Sebring: America's oldest endurance race. The organisers proudly state that "Our race only lasts half as long as the one in Daytona. But it is twice as painful." Insiders nod when they hear this. Several teams regard Sebring as the ideal test ahead of the 24 Hours of Le Mans. Especially because of the concrete slabs. Oh yes, and the present course, about six kilometres long, is partly made of concrete slabs with wide joints, so any racing car that is at all fragile is shaken to pieces.

The slabs date from the Second World War, when the US Army operated an airfield here. Immediately after the war, not a lot happened at Hendricks Army Airfield. Then, in 1950, the first racing cars zoomed across the concrete. On 15 March the starter's flag fell for the first 12-hour race. In the early years Porsche's small, light racing cars succeeded in annoying the "big boys". In 1960 Hans Herrmann and the Belgian driver Olivier Gende-bien gained a first overall win for Porsche in a 718 RS60 with a 1.6-litre engine and 160 hp. The car was quickly nicknamed "giant killer". In 1969 Porsche had to pay dues to the concrete: the 908/02 ran nice and easy at first, then the light space frames broke. The mechanics sawed flat pieces of iron out of the pits scaffolding and bolted them on the frames. Victory was lost, third place a poor consolation. Never to be forgotten is the second place of Steve McQueen/Peter Revson in 1970. McQueen drove his own 908/02 with a leg in plaster, following a motorbike accident!

Porsche has several records in the Sebring annals: 13 overall wins in succession, from 1976 to 1988; Derek Bell's lap record in a 962 in 1986 at 210.4 km/h, which has never been beaten; and 18 overall wins to date. The most recent victory, in 2008, went to an RS Spyder, which on paper was clearly inferior to its competitors – another giant killer.

___ Racing on an old army airstrip. The driver Jo Siffert is waiting for the start of the 12 Hours of Sebring by his short-tailed Porsche 907.

103— 1,000 Kilometres on the North Loop

Flying through the Eifel

The North Loop of the Nürburgring: a little over 20 kilometres through the hilly Eifel region. 170 bends, hills and valleys, summits and jumps, changes in road surface and crazy weather. Many people think this is the world's toughest racing track. Porsche won a major race here for the first time in 1967: the "1,000 kilometres". Joe Buzzetta and Udo Schütz pulled off this feat in a 910. In 1968 Vic Elford and Jo Siffert won in a 908.

Elford likes to tell stories that could only come from the Ring: "With the 908 we flew along the ›Brünnchen‹ section. You come through a right-hand bend from the Adenauer Bridge, followed by a few left curves, and then the climb up to the Carousel begins. On the way you are doing 270 through a gentle left curve where the road descends a bit for a short distance. We took off here. We were never very high off the ground, but because the road fell away, we were flying for 40 metres. That's not a problem – the 908 flew well." Elford and Jo Siffert won the race at a record average speed of 152.96 km/h. About the race in 1969, Elford says: "Later, in practice, I was driving a 908/02 ›Flounder‹, a flat, open racing car with 350 hp. The Flounder didn't fly well. As soon as I took off, the car's nose lifted. I slid along on the rear end until the front crashed down on the road again."

Porsche had a specially developed, highly agile racing car for orgies of bends like the North Loop: the 908/03 – which won there in 1970 and 1971. At the last 1,000-kilometre race on the North Loop in 1983, Stefan Bellof inscribed the Porsche name in the annals of the course: in qualifying on 28 May, he flew round the 20,832-kilometre track in a Porsche 956 in 6:11.13 minutes. The average speed was 202.073 km/h. This best time now stands for ever, just like Porsche's record of ten overall wins.

—— Never have so many racing cars been airborne as on the North Loop of the Nürburgring. Jo Siffert and Vic Elford won the 1,000-kilometre race in 1968 in this 908.

104__Le Mans

Toujour l'amour, sometimes fou

Porsche at Le Mans: well over 100 class wins, 19 overall victories and 18 best practice times. The win in 1971 came at an average speed of 222.3 km/h – a record that stood for 39 years. Porsche also booked the longest winning streak, from 1981 to 1987, and most cars in the top ten (nine in 1983).

The first turbo car in Le Mans was a Porsche in 1974, and the first winner with turbo was also a Porsche, in 1976. The first four-wheel drive was a Porsche, in 1986. In 2014 Porsche entered the 919 Hybrid featuring the most advanced hybrid drive, which charged the battery not only when braking, but also at full throttle via a turbine. Fielding the 919 Hybrid, Porsche pulled off a masterstroke, winning again in 2016 and 2017. Since the first Le Mans outing in 1951, Porsche sports cars have tackled the race on the Circuit du Mans 200 kilometres have competed every single year – in total 804 of them including 2019, which is also a record.

Porsche and Le Mans: big stories, and little anecdotes: how the first start in 1951 almost never happened because a mechanic smashed a 356 SL on the autobahn, the racing boss put a second one out of action when visiting Le Mans, while the third came to grief in practice – and the French drivers Auguste Veuillet and Edmond Mouche won in their class with a replacement car. How in 1957 Claude Storez pushed his Porsche 550 A Spyder to the finish for a whole hour, from the 23rd hour onwards, and celebrated seventh place but was disqualified. And Paul Frère, a legendary racing driver and journalist. In 1958 the weather was so terrible that Frère drove his 718 RSK Spyder into the pits in the night, frozen through, but warmed up so well that the little car gained first place in the category up to 1.5 litres, showing a clean pair of heels to several three-litre Ferraris.

___ The magnificent backdrop of Le Mans. The traditional Le Mans start, at which the drivers run across the finishing straight to their waiting cars, was held for the last time in 1969.

The pits at Le Mans
before the start in 1954.
Porsche is represented
by four 550 Spyders.
People are swarming all
over the finishing straight.

105_Paris–Dakar Rally

Entered Three Times, Won Twice

The Paris–Dakar Rally has been held since 1979, and 1984 saw the first win for a sports car: the Porsche 911 3.2 4x4, an ancestor of the four-wheel drive 911 for the road, which appeared in 1988. In 1985 Porsche took part again so that the 959 super sports car could prove itself over 14,000 kilometres of desert. To be exact: the transmission, bodywork and chassis – the engine was a normally aspirated 225hp-unit, as in the previous year. No Porsche finished the rally. In 1986 the 959 was entered with a water- and air-cooled four-valve twin turbo and 400 hp, plus the electronically controlled four-wheel-drive system. The result: a double victory.

Three Dakar rallies, and endless stories. In 1984 a collision with a cow failed to stop the eventual winner René Metge. Lack of sleep was as much part of the race as the sand. The mechanics drove behind the rally in trucks or flew from camp to camp, falling asleep on their feet in the aircraft. The engineer Roland Kussmaul, father of the rally car, drove one of the "racing service stations" and overturned twice – but got his Porsche to the finish. 1985 was a complete disaster: Jochen Mass rolled over his 959, Jacky Ickx rammed a rock, and an oil pipe ruptured in Metge's engine.

In 1986 they returned: Metge won ahead of Ickx, Kussmaul came in sixth in the chase car. Head of racing Peter Falk summed up 1986: "Living and working together under extremely basic conditions, the stress, fatigue, diarrhoea and colds demanded maximum adaptability, frugality, tolerance and willingness to help. There were no distinctions between drivers, engineers and mechanics. When two service vehicles were put out of action ... the situation was precarious, as half of the spare parts and four persons were no longer available. Thanks to a high level of discipline, morale and a touch of black humour, all difficulties were surmounted."

___ René Metge and Dominique Lemoyne won the Paris–Dakar Rally in 1984 with a 911 Carrera 3.2 4x4. It was the first time that Porsche competed in the desert marathon.

___ This looks like an adventure
– and that's what it is.
The 911 Carrera 3.2 4x4
reached 200 km/h
on level terrain like this
in the Sahara in 1984.

106__ Targa Florio

72 Kilometres, 800 Bends – per Lap

Today only sparrows populate the Tribune di Cerda. Otherwise it is quiet around the old pit lane and grandstands on the road near Cerda, a small town in northern Sicily. A nail is sticking out of the crumbling concrete of what was the Porsche pits – hammered in by racing boss Peter Falk in 1969 to hang up a wire for the radio system.

In this tranquil scene it is hard to imagine how thousands of spectators screamed and shouted when the Targa Florio racing cars thundered past or hurtled into the pits for refuelling. And when Alfa Romeos, Ferraris, Chaparrals, Lolas and Porsches accelerated out, their engines making an infernal noise, and set out on the next lap: 72 kilometres with 800 bends, narrow mountain roads going up to 700 metres and down again to the Buonfornello Straight by the sea, almost seven kilometres long. Practice took place in normal road traffic between donkey carts and trucks, full speed through crowded villages. Vincenzo Florio, initiator and organiser of the race, had warned the population: "It's better to lock up your children and domestic animals." The roads were reserved for the racers only on the day of the race itself.

From 1955 to 1973 the Targa Florio was a world championship event. In 1956 Porsche competed for the first time with the little 550A Spyder. The works team consisted of Huschke von Hanstein, head of press and racing, and his wife Ursula (catering), the mechanics Willi and Werner Enz, and the racing driver Umberto Maglioli. He left behind the big Maseratis, Ferraris and Mercedes in his tiny 550-kilogram car with 135 hp, and won. It was the first overall victory for Porsche in a major race. By 1973 there had been ten further wins. No marque won more often, and the lap record, set by the Finnish driver Leo Kinnunen in 1970 with the Porsche 908/03, will stand forever: 33 minutes, 36 seconds, average speed 128 km/h.

___ The racing driver Umberto Maglioli prepares for the start of the Targa Florio. It is 10 June 1956, and this will be the first overall victory for Porsche.

___ Here Herbert Müller is driving
a 911 Carrera RSR 2.8 to
victory in the Targa Florio
in 1973. This was that last year
that the road race was a
world championship event.

Many a Porsche victory was hard-fought, and many a race was lost in the last metres. Like with this 908 Longtail at Le Mans in 1969 ...

CLIFF-HANGERS

107__A Bike Pursuing a Porsche

A Burst Tyre at 175 km/h

Extreme sports of all kinds produce heroic stories, both happy and unhappy. Here is one that had a happy and an unhappy ending at one and the same time. It is about a Frenchman named Jean-Claude Rude, born in 1954, an extreme biker, as we would put it today.

After winning a few time-trials in Burgundy, Jean-Claude formed a plan to be the world's fastest cyclist. For this purpose he needed a decent slipstream. Porsche was open to the idea, and placed a gigantic spoiler about as big as a garden shed on the back of a Type 935. As on a pace-setting motorbike in a pacemaker race, there was a horizontal bar low down at the back of the Porsche. For ideal slipstreaming, Rude had to stay as close as possible to the bar. As the 800-hp twin turbo engine of the Porsche belched long flames from its exhaust when the engine load changed, the exhaust pipes were placed laterally. The man at the wheel of the Porsche was the racing driver Henri Pescarolo, who described the handling of the 935 with its spoiler as highly idiosyncratic. The aim was to be faster than the 204.8 km/h reached by the French cyclist José Meiffret, who had achieved this in 1962 on a closed-off stretch of the A5 autobahn near Freiburg, pedalling behind a Mercedes 300 SL.

The assets that Rude brought along were lots of courage, healthy lungs, strong legs and a bike that travelled 27 metres at every turn of the chain ring. In August 1978 the attempt started on the VW test track at Ehra-Lessien near Hanover, and everything was fine up to 175 km/h. Then Rude's back tyre burst. Unfortunately, this meant that the record attempt failed. Fortunately, the rider was unharmed. One and a half years later Jean-Claude Rude was in luck again when – this time without a Porsche – he fell at 150 km/h. In 1980 Jean-Claude's luck came to an end: he crashed while training in France and died.

____ In August 1978, the racing driver Henri Pescarolo (right), the daring Jean-Claude Rude and the 800-hp Porsche 935, starting out on Rude's speed-record attempt.

108__Le Mans 1969

24 Hours, 120 Metres Behind

It was Sunday, 15 June 1969: everyone who loved motor racing and could not be at Le Mans was glued to the television. The wobbly black-and-white views from the aircraft showed how Hans Herrmann in the little Porsche 908 and Jacky Ickx in the Ford GT40 were eating up the miles around the track. To see how the cars came close to each other, even touched, at unbelievable speeds or when they braked – this took away the breath of the watching fans. Finally came the footage of the home straight, with the GT40 whizzing past the man with the chequered flag after 24 hours, and the Porsche passing two seconds later. A difference of 120 metres after 24 hours.

For five hours the Porsche with the three-litre engine and the GT40 with the V8 five-litre whopper had battled it out. This duel came as a surprise, as the favourites were the new Porsche 917s, which set records in practice, did fabulous lap times and led in a league of their own until both were out of the race. Suddenly the GT40 and the 908 were vying for victory – which Herrmann and his team colleague Gérard Larrousse by no means took for granted. On the Saturday afternoon their 908 had already spent 35 minutes in the pits with a broken wheel bearing. Then the two of them took the bit between their teeth and chased the Ford until its lead vanished. Herrmann might have won the final combat against Ickx if the red warning light had not come on in the cockpit. When it lit up, this meant that the brake pads were worn out and he had to make a pit stop very quickly. Herrmann carried on driving for an hour with the light on in the cockpit, got the car round the course and possibly did not take every last risk. Know-all critics had their say.

A year later he returned and gained Porsche's first victory at Le Mans. In a dreadfully dangerous race in rain. Good drivers respond to criticism with their accelerator foot, they say.

___ "The Le Mans 120 Metres" – Jacky Ickx in a Ford GT40 beats Hans Herrmann driving a Porsche 908 by a whisker after a duel that has become legendary.

109__Daytona 1977:

No Door, but Lipstick on the Rear Lamp

For the constructors' world championship in 1977, Porsche had a new ace up its sleeve: the 2.85-litre engine of the 935 now got its air from two turbochargers instead of one, and was propelled with a mighty 630 hp. That is a lot for 790 kilograms of car.

In order to demonstrate this power-pack to American customers, Porsche sent the top drivers Jacky Ickx and Jochen Mass to the 24 Hours of Daytona in Florida with a 935. Mass did the fastest lap in practice, and Ickx made the fastest start to the race. Then Mass took over, and bad luck struck. A tyre burst in a fast bend and the 935 smashed into a wall. The oil radiator, a wheel and other parts were damaged, a door flew off. Mass managed to get the car to the pits, where it was repaired – but they had no new door. Never mind, after an hour Mass drove off without the door, which the stewards did not like. They made it clear to the Porsche crew that "Either you put a door in, or your car is out of the race." A customer donated the door of his 911. They carried on. Darkness arrived, and so did the guardians of the rule book: "Your rear lamp is missing … you can't continue like that." But Porsche people can improvise. They took a flashlight, coloured the glass with lipstick (where did that come from?) and stuck the light to the car.

On they went through the night, now in 42nd place. Mass and Ickx put on a unworldly display: the 935 flew round the track, cutting through the field like a hot knife through butter. As dawn broke, the Porsche was in second place, and men with puffy eyes in the pits scented victory. And then, with Mass in the car, a tyre burst in the banked curve, the 935 veered to the right – and lost everything that was sticking out, including both wheels. No, not quite everything: one wing mirror was still on the car. Mass was unharmed, but could not move the wreck one single inch further.

___ The end of an eventful drive in Daytona in 1977. The Porsche had hit a wall, and raced for a time with a door missing and equipped with a flashlight.

110__Le Mans 1977

Porsche's Only Victory with Five Cylinders

At the 24 Hours of Le Mans in 1976 Porsche had won in every class and took a first overall victory with a turbo engine. Renault could only stand and watch, and in 1977 entered a fighting force of four A 442 Turbos and two Mirage racing cars with works engines. Porsche answered with just two 936 Spyders and a 935.

On Saturday evening, a few hours after the start, the prospects were poor for the team from Stuttgart: a 936 Spyder and the 935 had dropped out with engine problems. The last 936 Spyder, driven by Jürgen Barth and Hurley Haywood, was in 42nd place, nine laps behind the leading Renault, after replacement of the injection pump. But Le Mans is a long race, and a lot can happen. And a lot did happen. At half past eight in the evening, racing boss Peter Falk put the Belgian Jacky Ickx into the remaining car as third driver. He was the man of the moment, putting in one record lap after another, once making repairs out on the course when a flat drive-belt for the injection pump came off, and only stopping for short breaks, while Barth maintained the hellish speed through rain and fog. The Renaults had to keep up, which took its toll on the cars from Dieppe. On Sunday afternoon the last A 442 Turbo was out of the race. Everything seemed decided now. After 23 hours the Porsche was 250 kilometres ahead of the second-placed car.

And then it happened – lots of smoke and no power. A piston had burned out. The mechanics removed the fuel injection from the damaged cylinder out in the pits, and the question now was: will our car make it around the course one more time? Because the rules say that to win, you have to cross the finishing line under your own steam after 24 hours. The race goes on until 4 pm on Sunday. Shortly before that time, Jürgen Barth climbed into the dying Porsche and coaxed the car round the course for two laps. Then Porsche had won this cliff-hanger.

____ The engine is dying, and tension runs high in the Porsche pits. Minutes before the end of the race, Jürgen Barth drove off. The engine held on and victory was assured in 1977.

111___Le Mans 1987

A Sweet Triumph in a Rough Year

Since 1982 Porsche had been unbeaten at Le Mans with the 956, then with the 962C, and until 1986 won the endurance world championship every year. But things got tough in 1987. Jaguar had become a strong opponent, beating Porsche one time after another. Before the Le Mans race, the British team was leading 4:0. However, Porsche wanted to show, at least for the 24-hour event, that the team and its ageing racing car was still one of the fastest.

At Weissach they assembled four 962Cs. One of them was wrecked their by Hans-Joachim Stuck in a test drive. His team colleague Price Cobb destroyed the second 962C in practice at Le Mans. So two remained for the race. Jochen Mass, Bob Wollek and Vern Schuppan took turns in the cockpit of the Porsche with number 18. Stuck, Derek Bell and Al Holbert were to tackle the marathon in the number 17. Marathon? Well, after an hour it was all over for number 18. A cylinder bank of the six-cylinder turbo machine was seriously damaged – the engine had been ruined by the low-quality fuel that the organisers supplied.

Now the Porsche team only had one car left in the race, with 23 hours to go and three Jaguars to beat. Saturday turned to Sunday, and as night fell, it started to drizzle. Stuck the Bavarian looked up at the clouds and rejoiced. He was not called the "rain king" for nothing. Stuck stayed in the cockpit for three hours. When he got out, he looked five years older and had taken a full lap's lead over the fastest Jaguar. At three o'clock on the Sunday morning, a Jaguar made a spectacular leap from the track following a burst tyre. Five hours later the second big cat took its leave with a faulty cylinder-head gasket, and the ailing third Jaguar drifted towards fifth place. Stuck, Bell and Holbert, however, held on to the end and won. It was a sweet triumph in a tough year.

___ Night is approaching and rain is about to fall. This is perfect weather for the Bavarian driver Stuck. He is in the car, ready to lay the foundations of victory with fabulous lap times.

Bibliographical information of the Deutsche Nationalbibliothek
The Deutsche Nationalbibliothek lists this publication
in the Deutsche Nationalbibliografie; detailed bibliographical
data are available on the internet at http://dnb.d-nb.de.

© Emons Verlag GmbH
© All illustrations: Historisches Archiv Porsche,
except no. 77: Gottfried Bechtold, Kunsthaus Bregenz
no. 72© Jeremy Cliff
© Cover design: mauritius images/Motoring Picture Library/Alamy
Layout: Jörg Weusthoff, Weusthoff Noël, Hamburg
based on a conception by Lübbeke | Naumann | Thoben

Printing and binding: Optimal Media, Röbel/Müritz
English translation: John Sykes, Cologne
ISBN 978-3-7408-0035-2

The publisher would like to thank the Historisches Archiv Porsche, especially
Jens Torner, for making images available and for excellent cooperation.

Reprint 2020, 5th edition
For the latest information about emons,
subscribe to our regular newsletter at
www.emons-verlag.de

For more than three decades *Wilfried Müller*
has been writing about cars, about people who
make cars, and about daredevils who drive
them. Born in Cologne, he travelled around the
world for many years as a motor-sports repor-
ter, later wrote numerous books and discovered
his passion for Porsche, a theme that occupies
him to this day. Wilfried Müller lives in New
Zealand with his wife and two children.